The United Nations: Structure for Peace

Some Publications of the
COUNCIL ON FOREIGN RELATIONS

FOREIGN AFFAIRS (quarterly), edited by Hamilton Fish Armstrong.

THE UNITED STATES IN WORLD AFFAIRS (annual). Volumes for 1931, 1932 and 1933, by Walter Lippmann and William O. Scroggs; for 1934-1935, 1936, 1937, 1938, 1939 and 1940, by Whitney H. Shepardson and William O. Scroggs; for 1945-1947, 1947-1948 and 1948-1949, by John C. Campbell; for 1949, 1950, 1951, 1952, 1953 and 1954, by Richard P. Stebbins; for 1955, by Hollis W. Barber; for 1956, 1957, 1958, 1959, and 1960 by Richard P. Stebbins.

DOCUMENTS ON AMERICAN FOREIGN RELATIONS (annual). Volume for 1952 edited by Clarence W. Baier and Richard P. Stebbins; for 1953 and 1954, edited by Peter V. Curl; for 1955, 1956, 1957, 1958 and 1959, edited by Paul E. Zinner; or 1960 edited by Richard P. Stebbins.

POLITICAL HANDBOOK OF THE WORLD (annual), edited by Walter H. Mallory.

ARMS AND POLITICS IN LATIN AMERICA (Revised Edition), by Edwin Lieuwen.

THE FUTURE OF UNDERDEVELOPED COUNTRIES: Political Implications of Economic Development (Revised Edition), by Eugene Staley.

SPAIN AND DEFENSE OF THE WEST: Ally and Liability, by Arthur P. Whitaker.

SOCIAL CHANGE IN LATIN AMERICA TODAY: Its Implications for United States Policy, by Richard N. Adams, John P. Gillin, Allan R. Holmberg, Oscar Lewis, Richard W. Patch, and Charles W. Wagley.

FOREIGN POLICY: THE NEXT PHASE: The 1960s (Revised Edition), by Thomas K. Finletter.

DEFENSE OF THE MIDDLE EAST: Problems of American Policy (Revised Edition), by John C. Campbell.

COMMUNIST CHINA AND ASIA: Challenge to American Policy, by A. Doak Barnett.

FRANCE, TROUBLED ALLY: De Gaulle's Heritage and Prospects, by Edgar S. Furniss, Jr.

THE SCHUMAN PLAN: A Study in Economic Cooperation, 1950-1959, by William Diebold, Jr.

SOVIET ECONOMIC AID: The New Aid and Trade Policy in Underdeveloped Countries, by Joseph S. Berliner.

RAW MATERIALS: A Study of American Policy, by Percy W. Bidwell.

NATO AND THE FUTURE OF EUROPE, by Ben T. Moore.

AFRICAN ECONOMIC DEVELOPMENT, by William A. Hance.

INDIA AND AMERICA: A Study of Their Relations, by Phillips Talbot and S. L. Poplai.

JAPAN BETWEEN EAST AND WEST, by Hugh Borton, Jerome B. Cohen, William J. Jorden, Donald Keene, Paul F. Langer and C. Martin Wilbur.

NUCLEAR WEAPONS AND FOREIGN POLICY, by Henry A. Kissinger.

MOSCOW-PEKING AXIS: Strengths and Strains, by Howard L. Boorman, Alexander Eckstein, Philip E. Mosely and Benjamin Schwartz.

CLIMATE AND ECONOMIC DEVELOPMENT IN THE TROPICS, by Douglas H. K. Lee.

WHAT THE TARIFF MEANS TO AMERICAN INDUSTRIES, by Percy W. Bidwell.

UNITED STATES SHIPPING POLICY, by Wytze Gorter.

RUSSIA AND AMERICA: Dangers and Prospects, by Henry L. Roberts.

STERLING: Its Meaning in World Finance, by Judd Polk.

KOREA: A Study of U.S. Policy in the United Nations, by Leland M. Goodrich.

FOREIGN AFFAIRS BIBLIOGRAPHY, 1942-1952, by Henry L. Roberts.

AMERICAN AGENCIES INTERESTED IN INTERNATIONAL AFFAIRS, compiled by Ruth Savord and Donald Wasson.

JAPANESE AND AMERICANS: A Century of Cultural Relations, by Robert S. Schwantes.

The United Nations: Structure for Peace

by

ERNEST A. GROSS

Published for the
Council on Foreign Relations
by
New York · HARPER & BROTHERS · *1962*

The Council on Foreign Relations is a non-profit institution devoted to study of the international aspects of American political, economic and strategic problems. It takes no stand, expressed or implied, on American policy. The authors of books published under the auspices of the Council are responsible for their statements of fact and expressions of opinion. The Council is responsible only for determining that they should be presented to the public.

138279

In Memory of Dag Hammarskjold

"When Societies First Come to Birth, it is the Leaders who Produce the Institutions. . . . Later, it is the Institutions which Produce the Leaders."

Montesquieu.

Policy Books of the Council on Foreign Relations

With the publication of this volume the Council on Foreign Relations inaugurates a new series of short books on important issues of U.S. foreign policy. The purpose is twofold: first, to provide readers in this country and elsewhere with analytical studies of the highest quality on problems of world significance; and second, to contribute to constructive thinking on American policies for the future. These volumes will make a virtue of brevity, without oversimplification, presenting concisely the reasoned conclusions of authors with first-hand experience and special qualifications.

The Council was fortunate in persuading Ernest A. Gross, who has represented the United States at the United Nations with distinction and has an intimate knowledge of the world organization, to undertake the writing of this book. In the course of its preparation Mr. Gross had the benefit of the advice and comments of a special group invited to review and discuss the manuscript. The Council wishes to thank the following, who were members of that group, for giving their time and their counsel: Joseph E. Johnson (Chairman), Hamilton Fish Armstrong, Harding F. Bancroft, James P. Baxter, 3rd, Lincoln P. Bloomfield, John C. Campbell, Lawrence S. Finkelstein, George S. Franklin, Jr., Leland M. Goodrich, H. Field Haviland, Jr., James N. Hyde, Elmore Jackson, Philip C. Jessup, Carl Marcy, Charles Burton Marshall, Charles Phelps Noyes and Christopher H. Phillips. John C. Campbell, who is in charge of the new series of short policy studies, edited the book and steered it to completion.

Responsibility for the statements of fact and opinion rests with the author, not with the group or the Council. The Council takes responsibility for the decision to publish the book as a contribution to thought on a subject of the greatest moment; the future of the United Nations and its importance for American foreign policy.

Contents

The United Nations:
Structure for Peace

Introduction

Framework for a Just Peace

The United Nations combines a code of international conduct with a machinery for giving it practical effect.

When the San Francisco Conference met in 1945, every delegation present spoke for a nation still at war. The battlefield of Europe had already counted more than fourteen million dead. Furthermore, it was understood "that another war would be fought, if there were another war, with weapons capable of reaching every part of the earth—that similar weapons had indeed been brought to the point of use in the present conflict." [1]

Appraisal of the "spirit of San Francisco" should take into account its wartime mood and setting. The nations there assembled were indeed united, pursuing the most common of all human interests: survival.

Notwithstanding occasional warnings that the Charter is "pre-atomic"—a comment which could, with equal irrelevance, be made about the U.S. Constitution—few delegates at San Francisco had illusions concerning the perils and challenges ahead. Soviet intransigence had already begun to arouse grave doubt concerning the validity of Winston Churchill's prediction in 1943 that, after the war, "the most intense effort will be made by the leading powers to prolong their honorable association," which was also an assumption of American policy.

[1] Secretary of State Edward R. Stettinius, Jr., "Report to the President on the Results of the San Francisco Conference" (June 26, 1945), in *The Charter of the United Nations,* Hearings before the Senate Committee on Foreign Relations, 79th Cong., 1st sess., July 9-13, 1945 (Washington: GPO, 1945; rev.), pp. 35-36.

3

It is not clear why the Soviet Union should have thought it expedient to join the United Nations in the first place. The Charter, which defines the cooperative interests of free and independent societies, is the antithesis of the Communist doctrine, which goes no further than to tolerate "coexistence" as a transition to Soviet hegemony. The Soviet Union's efforts to subvert the Organization to its own uses have shown from the beginning that its adherence to the Charter was rooted in a cynical interpretation of self-interest.

The surprising adaptability of the United Nations to changing needs over the years must sometimes raise doubts in the Kremlin concerning the Organization's role in Soviet foreign policy, at least as anxious as doubts which occasionally beset the United States. Soviet leaders today may wonder whether Soviet membership in the United Nations was not, after all, another Stalin blunder, a consequence of the "illusions of San Francisco."

Nevertheless, the Soviet Union has stayed in, perhaps fearing that its withdrawal might not merely break up the Organization, but also convert the remnants into an anti-Soviet coalition. Those in our own country who may be led by fear or frustration to urge American withdrawal from the United Nations should likewise ponder the risk that such action on our part might not only relinquish leadership, but indeed transfer it to the enemies of freedom.

It is, of course, not enough to argue that the United States should remain in the Organization merely because, or so long as, the Soviet Union does so. We should lose no time in exercising our right of withdrawal if American vital national interests were in fact impaired by adherence to the Charter. Conclusions as to the advantages or disadvantages of U.S. membership in the United Nations must be based upon realistic appraisal of some inescapable questions.

First and foremost, what is the relationship between the purposes of the Charter and the objectives of U.S. policy? How can United Nations processes be most effectively used to carry out the Charter, even while the world goes through a dangerous, and indefinitely prolonged, period of conflict and adjustment? And how can the United States make better use of the means provided by the United Nations: to marshal mutual support for tasks we believe must be done in our own and in the common interest; to advance the general objectives both of our foreign policy and those of the Charter; and to strengthen the Organization itself, so that it can, in the atomic age, help us to deter aggression or, if aggression should occur, repress it without a suicidal holocaust?

The development of new weapons and delivery systems confronts the members, both great and small, with dilemmas which could not have been foreseen at San Francisco.

The Charter sanctions the right of self-defense only against "armed attack" (Article 51). Today, when armed attack is deterred by fear of atomic reprisal, aggression is more likely to take less overt forms, such as subversion, fraud or duress. Despite the Charter's limitation to "armed attack," however, few would deny legitimacy to self-defense against these forms of aggression in the event of the failure of the United Nations to protect members against them.

Nevertheless, collective action against indirect aggression, in all its undefinable varieties, is far from assured. Advanced systems of order punish all acts which the group treats as crimes. Rudimentary systems—such as the United Nations—treat as crimes only those acts which the group is prepared to punish. The list of punishable offenses tends to shrink, in proportion to the growth of atomic might in the hands of potential aggressors. Deterrence is itself deterred by fear.

On the other hand, the international community is changing in ways which enlarge areas of common interest fully as much as they increase common terror. New nations explode into being, not like stars in space, but as neighbors on a crowded planet. Developments in science, technology, transport and communication release forces latent in individuals and groups.

The opening words of the Charter—"We the peoples of the United Nations, determined to save succeeding generations from the scourge of war. . . ."—reflected the far-ranging hopes of 1945. Today, there is a sense of urgent immediacy in saving our own generation, to say nothing of succeeding ones.

The Charter treats as menaces to peace the ancient enemies of all mankind: ignorance, poverty and disease. The United Nations thus marks an advance over the Covenant of the League of Nations, which did not ignore these deeper sources of tension yet tended in practice to equate peace with mere avoidance of violence. The members of the League accepted the principle that suppression of aggression is public business. Nevertheless, economic and social causes of unrest and disorder were widely regarded as matters of essentially domestic, rather than international, concern.

The Charter reflects a lesson of history: peace can be maintained only by giving it organization and structure. The Pax Romana and the Pax Britannica were effective not because they were alternatives to force—which was used freely to enforce the Pax. They had a survival value because the imperial instinct provided a framework for the peace.

As a declaration of principles for giving shape to durable peace, the United Nations Charter leaves little to be desired. It would be difficult—and unnecessary—to compose a better one. Its potential value, however, lies in its offer of both a set of rules and a set of tools. In combination, these provide the rudiments of a collective security system.

Traditional usage of the term "collective security" stresses the object of marshaling sufficient force to deter or repress violent changes in the *status quo*. A realistic appraisal of the working requirements of such an effort, however, should give equal weight to its positive quality as well. Unless remedies for wrongs exist, and orderly change is assured when justice requires, then what passes for a system of collective *security* to maintain *peace* is more likely to be a system of collective *repression* to maintain *order*—a reincarnation of the Holy Alliance.

"Collective security" may be defined as a system which assures that illicit ends cannot be achieved by any means, whereas legitimate ends can be achieved by proper means.

What matters, of course, is how and whether abstract concepts such as "illicit ends" and "proper means" are given content in concrete cases. Violence should always be hopeless; a just cause, never.

It follows that the effective functioning of any system of true collective security—even in the primitive form which marks the limits of our present capacity for achievement—requires:

(1) a broad agreement upon principles as to which ends and means are legitimate and which are not, (2) available machinery for applying the principles to specific situations, and (3) a general will to use the machinery.

The principles are furnished by the Charter. The machinery is provided in the structure and processes of the Organization. The will can be supplied only by the members.

Even though the United Nations is neither a power nor a parliament, it is, in the words of the late Secretary-General, "a framework for diplomatic operations." As such, the Organization has, from the outset, been regarded not as an exclusive mechanism but one "supplementary to all the other machinery of international relationships, rather than one that would entirely supplant the latter." [2]

Whether the United Nations was "oversold" in the first place, or merely misunderstood, its essential capabilities could in any event be determined only through trial and error. At the end of his thirty-year term as Chief Justice, John Marshall was moved, by intense factionalism within our country, to write to a colleague: "I yield slowly and reluctantly to the conviction that our Constitution cannot last." Today, ours is the oldest of all written constitutions, because of its adaptability and the wisdom of those who guided its use, including the great Chief Justice himself. It was, after all, not the Constitution that was on trial; it was the capacity for self-discipline of an emerging community of states.

Similarly, the survival value of the United Nations must be evaluated according to the manner of its use, rather than

[2] Leo Pasvolsky, Address at the University of Illinois, May 2, 1950. Dr. Pasvolsky was one of the principal draftsmen of the Charter.

the volume of its business. Mischief is done to the Organization when it is leaned on as a crutch—rather than employed
as an instrument—of diplomacy. The United Nations cannot
serve as a substitute for national policy, any more than a
hospital can replace a public health system. Whether the
Organization is used as a first or a last resort in crisis, "failures" attributed to it inexorably register the difficulties encountered by the members in reaching agreement or solution
in specific cases.

It is observable that some in our country who assail the
United Nations as a menacing "superstate" are often first to
deride it for not acting like one in situations of particular
moment to the United States. On the other extreme are those
who make vague appeals for "support to the United Nations,"
thus claiming for it an abstract or corporate existence it does
not in fact possess. The "support" needed is that of informed
public pressures for more effective use of the machinery established by sovereign states which are voluntary parties to a
treaty called the "Charter of the United Nations."

American attitudes toward the Organization often reflect
the moral dilemmas and balances of risk confronting a nation
whose responsibilities are greater than its capacity to shape
events. By and large—despite occasional slogans implying love
of power for its own sake—the United States has tried to act
in the spirit of Admiral Mahan's prescription of statecraft
and strategy: "It is the function of force to give moral ideas
time to take root." But the international climate appears in-
hospitable to "moral ideas," and the roots have found only a
tenuous hold in a divided world.

Public controversy and concern arise as to our future course.
Some insist we play a lone hand; others, a free hand; still
others, a strong hand. Many would narrow our circles of interest and responsibility, warning against dangers in shaping our
policies in deference to some dimly defined "world opinion."

Confidence is shaken also by the refusal of some smaller nations to take positions on clear-cut issues of principle. A prime
example was that of the failure of the governments assembled
at Belgrade in September 1961 to react sharply to the Soviet

resumption of nuclear testing on the eve of the conference. Their inaction certainly did nothing to discourage the Soviet government from carrying to its grim conclusion the policy of manifesto by megaton. Obviously the Soviet government had used ostensible negotiations with the Western powers as a cover to prepare for action which was the very subject at issue.

Notwithstanding their refusal to condemn such a perversion of the negotiating process, the conferees at Belgrade nevertheless declared, in tones of ringing abstraction, that "there is no choice between negotiations and war." So obvious a failure to relate clear principle to specific cases has led many in the United States to fear that the policies of small nations are not merely nonaligned politically, so much as out of alignment with reality.

It would, nevertheless, be an error to react in anger and assert that any who do not "stand up to be counted" are summarily to be counted out. For one thing, the nations which accepted invitations to the Belgrade Conference did not by any means comprise all the states whose foreign policies are based on nonalignment. Of all Latin America, only Cuba participated. Only one-third of the independent African states attended, and approximately one-half of the Asian states. Yugoslavia was the only government represented from the entire continent of Europe. Moreover, those who did attend formed a disparate grouping, divided by much more than united them, finding it difficult to agree on a conference report, and taking pains to deny any intention to make a "bloc."

Communist insistence that such a bloc nevertheless exists is designed to portray a fragmented world in which nations confront a choice of "sides," rather than of principles. In this connection, the United States and its Western allies should heed a warning once voiced by Hamilton Fish Armstrong with respect to Japan, and which has wider validity as well: "If the Japanese could be brought to lump the Soviet Union and the United States together in suspicion and dislike, that would represent a tremendous Soviet advance." [3]

[3] "Japan at Cross-Purposes," *Foreign Affairs*, January 1956, p. 233.

One warning signal of such degeneration in the relative American position is the extent to which the cold war becomes less widely regarded throughout the world as a Soviet revolt against the Charter, and more as a power duel between two giants, with the smaller nations looking on as bystanders or hanging on as clients.

The fact is that conflicts between the great powers rarely, if ever, involve matters limited only to their own direct interests. The deep concerns of third parties may be hidden, or even disclaimed. Yet, few nations would willingly give to others a power of attorney to settle issues involving their own destiny. With respect to such issues, the general experience is that, though governments may be uncommitted in public, they are rarely noncommittal in private.

In sum, new forces, new states, and new power relationships have made it more important for all members of the United Nations to use the Organization more effectively. Accomplishment of the Charter objectives becomes more—not less—vital, as Communist power increases and danger of conflict is heightened by the incessant Soviet revolt against the Charter.

New opportunities bring need for corresponding changes in process and structure. These include more effective exercise of authority by the popular parliamentary organ—the General Assembly—together with expanded powers for the executive organ—the Secretary-General. These two developments are inevitably linked. Unless the General Assembly's right to recommend is supplemented by the Secretary-General's capacity to act, no practicable means exist for the General Assembly to discharge its responsibilities for peace, when the Security Council is veto-bound. Hence, Soviet proposals to impair the United Nations' capacity for executive action must be regarded as blows aimed at the United Nations itself.

In addition to the requirements for change in structure and process, which are related primarily to *keeping* the peace, it is necessary to analyze the nature of the problems which must be faced in building the foundations of international order.

Peace is a condition of the human society, just as health is a condition of the human organism. Neither is ever permanently "achieved"; both must be sustained through the application of creative will. The history of man is the history of endless struggle toward durable peace and a just order.

In evaluating the United Nations as a framework for this ageless effort, the following discussion is divided into two parts. The first deals in the main with organized processes for keeping the peace; the second is concerned with problems involved in building the foundations of a just order.

The discussion attempts to appraise the record of the United Nations—and, more particularly, that of the United States in the Organization—in furthering these twin objectives. Even more boldly, it endeavors to suggest ways in which the United Nations might be employed more effectively in the struggle toward a just and stable order among nations.

Part I

KEEPING THE PEACE

Chapter I

The Secretary-General—
as Guardian of the Peace

The death of Dag Hammarskjold, in the African night, brought into focus a dilemma which the nations had long confronted but never squarely faced.

Experience had shown that an impartial and vigorous executive might help prevent situations such as Suez and the Congo from engulfing the world in great-power conflict. On the other hand, a great power can start a conflict any time it is determined to do so. Hence, to the extent that the Secretary-General himself becomes a source of controversy among the great powers, his capacity to exert a conciliating influence among them obviously diminishes.

Through qualities of strength and firmness, the late Secretary-General had sustained the precarious principle of executive impartiality, around which the smaller nations huddled, but did not rally. His passing precipitated the necessity for choice.

Would the smaller nations, over Soviet objection, insist upon action enabling the United Nations to develop its integral growth and corporate processes? Or would the Organization become a mere cold war meeting ground, like the springs at which hostile Indian tribes assembled for intervals of healing between wars?

The Choice of a Successor

In the event, the membership temporized. The Sixteenth General Assembly opened its session on the day following Mr. Hammarskjold's death. The Assembly stood in solemn tribute, then speedily recessed. When it reassembled, no member took the initiative. Some delegates, in response to the mood and need of the moment, thought the Assembly should at once request its newly elected President, Mongi Slim of Tunisia, to undertake a temporary observation over the affairs of the Secretariat. He could have done so ex officio, without a title, and pending appointment of a regular or acting Secretary-General in accordance with the Charter. It was their view that the Assembly could and should discharge its responsibility to ensure the uninterrupted functioning of the Secretariat, which the Charter establishes as a principal organ of the United Nations (Article 7).

Exercise by the President of the General Assembly of such a responsibility might have afforded a useful experiment in strengthening coordination between Assembly and Secretariat. As an interim arrangement, it would not have involved an undue "parliamentary" encroachment upon the executive. Its sole purpose would have been to assure continuity of Secretariat operations in the interest of the whole membership. The Assembly would have retained freedom to withdraw or modify the mandate, just as the Security Council at any time could have asserted its Charter prerogative to recommend a Secretary-General for appointment by the Assembly.

It is never possible to replay the record of an event. Immediate exertion by the United States of maximum pressures, without allowing time for extended consultations with and among the bewildered delegations, might have aroused resentment. On the other hand, delay entailed another familiar risk: loss of direction due to lack of leadership. The latter risk was all the more serious in light of the fact that a committee of eight "experts" from various nations had only recently found itself deadlocked, despite a year-long effort, to agree on methods of revising the Secretariat structure.

In an earlier struggle over the Secretariat—when the Soviets in 1950 attempted to unseat Trygve Lie because he had opposed Communist aggression in Korea—the United States had put a stop to incipient rivalry and confusion by threatening to use the veto, if necessary, to block any other candidate.

The situation which arose in the aftermath of Mr. Hammarskjold's death was too complex to permit of so blunt a tactic. Mr. Slim was himself widely regarded as a candidate for the office of Secretary-General, making it all the more difficult to request him to assume a caretaker's role while President of the Assembly. Improvised groupings of smaller nations, broadly representative of the world's geographical areas, undertook to find a formula with which the members, including the United States and the Soviet Union, might concur.

With few exceptions, the members stood firm against the Soviet proposal for a triumvirate. The late Secretary-General had left a double legacy: a functioning Secretariat, which was able to carry on its business through weeks of stalemate, and an awareness among the smaller nations that their interests called for an efficient and vigorous executive arm of the Organization.

The Soviet Union grudgingly receded from a position which obviously commanded no general respect. Although the headlines focused on closed sessions between the United States and Soviet delegations, it was the smaller powers which at last found a basis for accord.

However, the formula under which U Thant was unanimously chosen as Acting Secretary-General contained a time bomb, set to explode April 10, 1963—the end of what would have been Mr. Hammarskjold's regular term. So short a tenure, coupled with Mr. Thant's undertaking to work in a spirit of "mutual understanding" with his subordinates, threatens harm to the independence of the office. The chief executive is not relieved of personal responsibility, yet is subjected to a constraint which may either deter him from action or make him more vulnerable to attack if he should risk action.

The ambiguity implicit in the compromise is not the fault

of draftsmanship. It follows from an effort to preserve the principle of a vigorous executive with a formula which might —unless carefully applied—prove to be inconsistent with the working requirements of such a function. Appraisal of the significance of the formula is relevant not as a criticism of what has been done, but as a means of weighing the future course the United States should pursue. Barring unpredictable developments, such as Soviet abandonment of the troika, the dilemma will recur at the Seventeenth General Assembly in the fall of 1962, in anticipation of the expiration of U Thant's term in April of the following year.

It is impossible to predict how the present formula will be applied in practice, the form in which the matter may arise at the next session, or its political context. Nevertheless, it is these very uncertainties which make it essential to understand the principle at stake and to employ all the arts and pressures of our diplomacy in the intervening period to make clear our insistence that there be no paltering with the principle.

Powers and Duties

The principle, simply stated, is insulation of the Secretariat (the Secretary-General and his entire staff) from governmental pressures. The suggestion was made at the San Francisco Charter Conference that the Secretary-General should have five deputies, elected by the Assembly on the recommendation of the Security Council. The proposal was abandoned by its sponsors, including the Soviet Delegation, as a result of arguments effectively stressing the need for a single responsible officer. The principle of personal responsibility was emphasized; the "idea of a 'Cabinet system' in which responsibility for the administration and political functions would be distributed among several individuals was squarely rejected." [1]

Hence the commitment by the Acting Secretary-General that he will collaborate and consult with his subordinates "in a

[1] Address by Mr. Hammarskjold at Oxford University (May 30, 1961), U.N. Press Release SG/1035.

spirit of mutual understanding" before taking action,[2] may prove to be retrogressive.

In discharging his duties, a Secretary-General must choose between two courses of action. He might "refuse to indicate a stand in emerging conflicts, in order thus to preserve the neutrality of office." This, Mr. Hammarskjold described as "negative neutrality." Or, he might make "an independent but positive evaluation, free of partisan influences and determined by the Charter." This course, he once said, "builds up a practice which may open the door to a more generally recognized independent influence for the Organization as such in the political evolution." [3]

The Charter leaves no room for doubt that its framers expected the office to bear the broader responsibility. Article 99 authorizes the Secretary-General to "bring to the attention of the Security Council any matter which in his opinion may threaten the maintenance of international peace and security." Thus, the Secretary-General and Secretariat as a "principal organ" of the United Nations, is granted a right also conferred, in virtually identical language, upon the General Assembly (Article 11 [3]).

The importance of this power was well understood by the authors of the Charter, inasmuch as experience of the League of Nations had shown the dangers of delay when only the members had the right to bring threatening situations to the notice of the Council. Even prior to the San Francisco Conference, the Soviet and American governments had agreed that delegating the right would be "a very useful procedure when no member of the Organization wishes to take the initiative." Just this happened, for example, when the Security Council was convened at Mr. Hammarskjold's request on July 14, 1960, in order to deal with the first major crisis in the series of crises which have made up the "Congo problem."

On the principle that a broad grant of power includes a lesser one, the Secretary-General properly asserted that his

[2] Statement by Acting Secretary-General U Thant, U.N. Press Release SG/1060, November 3, 1960.

[3] Address at Copenhagen (May 1, 1959), U.N. Press Release SG/812.

right under Article 99 also carried with it the power to investigate and observe conditions on the spot, personally or through his chosen representatives. Pursuant to this principle, he visited Laos in November 1959 at the request of the Laotian government. This later drew Soviet fire as an unneutral and unauthorized action. It is to be expected that in future the new Acting Secretary-General will be strongly "advised" by his Soviet subordinate against similar action in other cases.

The right to call to the attention of the Security Council any "matter" threatening peace is not limited to *disputes* among members. It extends with like force to conflict-breeding conditions and to underlying social and economic sources of tension.

Closely related to this right is the duty of the Secretary-General under Article 98 of the Charter to perform functions entrusted to him by the General Assembly, the Security Council, the Economic and Social Council and the Trusteeship Council, as well as to make an annual report to the General Assembly on the work of the Organization. The combination of these duties embodies the essential executive functions, in addition to administration, of supplying information, admonition and advice. His reports should be designed to remind the members of past failures as well as accomplishments, and should frankly point out the progress still to be made.

Here again, the greater right must be deemed to include a lesser. Submission of annual reports has made apparent the desirability of special reports covering specific matters of concern to the membership. Such reports, both regular and special, have value only to the extent they reflect independent and objective judgment of the Secretary-General. If such reports were distilled, through a process of "consultation," to a mere reflection of negative neutrality, the Organization would be deprived of a major source of invigoration.

Moreover, the Secretary-General bears responsibility for supervising a perpetual diplomatic conference, which characterizes the United Nations as a framework both for negotiations and operations. Accordingly, Secretariat responsibilities include: negotiation of agreements; mediation and good offices; strategic missions of police or paramilitary character; administration of scientific, economic, cultural, legal and public information programs.

Effective discharge of such a range of duties—monitoring dangerous situations, reporting his views and recommending improvements in procedures, supervising a continuous conference, carrying on private diplomacy, and carrying out mandates of the Assembly and Security Council—all these functions necessitate freedom for the executive to act independently within the provisions of the Charter and the mandates of the political organs.

The principle for which the late Secretary-General stood is embodied in Article 100 of the Charter, prohibiting the Secretariat staff from seeking or receiving instructions from any government and enjoining upon members a duty "to respect the exclusively international character" of the Secretariat responsibilities. The Soviet government joined in sponsoring the doctrine as early as the Dumbarton Oaks Conference in 1944.

Several months prior to his death, Mr. Hammarskjold warned that, as a principle, this was not negotiable. He referred to a tendency, which he perceived even in some "Western circles," to retreat from the doctrine of an international Secretariat toward the concept of an intergovernmental one, on the misguided theory that, because the Soviet government was hostile to the former, its continuance would increase tensions which it was the purpose of the United Nations to diminish. Such a retreat, he warned: ". . . might well prove to be the Munich of international cooperation. . . . To abandon or compromise with principles on which such cooperation is built may be no less dangerous than to compromise with principles regarding the rights of a nation. In both cases the price to be paid may be peace." [4]

The principle embodied in Article 100 of the Charter is enacted in the First Article of the Staff Regulations, the internal law of the Secretariat of the United Nations: "Members

[4] Address at Oxford University (May 30, 1961), cited.

of the Secretariat are international civil servants. Their responsibilities are not national, but exclusively international. By accepting appointment, they pledge themselves to discharge their functions and to regulate their conduct with the interests of the United Nations only in view." [5]

The principle is under siege by the Soviet government, which insists that men cannot respond to a general morality, because "the capitalist world has its own moral standards, the Communist world its own, and the neutralist countries their own." [6] This is an echo, across forty years of Communist history, of Lenin's dictum of 1920: "Our morality is deduced from the class struggle of the proletariat, and Communist morality is the morality which serves this struggle." It is an outlook unintelligible to ethical concepts grounded in any of the world's major religious faiths.

Mr. Hammarskjold was asked at a press conference to comment on the Soviet contention that objectivity is irreconcilable with the workings of the mind and that there can be no "neutral" individuals. He undertook to respond in personal terms: "It may be true that in a very deep, human sense there is no neutral individual because everyone, if he is worth anything, has to have his ideas and ideals. . . . But what I do claim is that even a man who is in that sense not neutral can very well undertake and carry through neutral actions, because that is an act of integrity. . . . 'Neutrality' may develop, after all, into a kind of *jeu de mots*. I am not neutral as regards facts. But that is not what we mean. What is meant by 'neutrality' in this kind of debate is, of course, neutrality in relation to interests. . . ." [7]

[5] Staff Regulations of March 1, 1952, G.A. Resolution 590 (VI), February 2, 1952, U.N. General Assembly (6th sess.), *Official Records: Supplement 20, Resolutions Adopted During . . . 6 November 1951-5 February 1952*, A/2119 (New York: Author, 1952), p. 76. (Hereafter the General Assembly's *Official Records* will be cited as G.A.O.R., and those of the Security Council as S.C.O.R. The place of publication and publisher of these, as well as of other General Assembly or Security Council documents, will be New York and the issuing organization.)

[6] Nikita S. Khrushchev, Address before the U.N. General Assembly (October 3, 1960); complete text in *The New York Times*, October 4, 1960.

[7] June 12, 1961; Note no. 2347.

It is indeed difficult to regard as more than cynical word play a suggestion that the individual is so conditioned by his society that he cannot make objective judgments concerning politically controversial matters. The life of Boris Pasternak reveals that even in the most repressive systems individuals remain capable of diversity and dissent.

The Soviet effort to corrode the concept of an international service as such is likely to harm the Organization in unsuspected ways. For one thing, it involves an insidious assault upon the integrity of loyal and devoted civil servants, whose careers are pledged in good faith to observance of the basic principle of the Staff Regulations. Not only is the self-confidence of the staff undermined by external suspicion and internal dissension. Even worse, first-rate talent will not long be available for recruitment into a demoralized service. The spring is poisoned at the source.

Moreover, regarding the matter from the U.S. point of view, a Soviet campaign of lies has tended to discredit American officials on the Secretariat. If the members of the United Nations are induced to believe that these officials supinely respond to orders from the U.S. government, who is then to criticize the Soviet Union for insisting upon a similar privilege with respect to its own nationals serving the Secretariat?

Furthermore, although Americans have in the past served with distinction as Directors of several Specialized Agencies,[8] the International Telecommunications Union and the International Labor Organization alone now have American Directors-General, and there are not likely to be more in the future, if the current attitudes of members persist.

Members of the United Nations are quite agreeable to the United States assuming major financial and logistical burdens of the Organization. Nevertheless, the same nations are equally ready to indulge the fiction that, if qualified Americans assumed positions of high responsibility in more than token numbers, the United Nations would become engulfed by the

---

[8] UNESCO and International Atomic Energy Agency, among others. The International Bank has an American president, but the Soviet Union is not a member.

cold war. A false equivalence is thus drawn between service on the Secretariat by American and Soviet nationals despite the fact that the Soviet Union has never borne its fair share of the Organization's financial burdens, has rarely made its first talents available for service notwithstanding frequent bids by the Secretary-General to do so, and has rejected the principle of an international civil service.

Evolution of the Office

The evolution of the office of the Secretary-General has reflected, from the very first year of the Organization's existence, the inadequacy of a mere "static conference machinery" and the need for a "dynamic instrument of Governments . . . for increasingly effective forms of active international cooperation. . . ." [9] The struggle over the nature and scope of the executive function involves a calculated choice between these two concepts.

Attitudes of the great powers toward this matter have by no means been clear or consistent since 1946. In that year, for example, when Iran complained to the Security Council of Soviet interference in the internal affairs of Iran, Secretary-General Lie entered into a controversy between the U.S.S.R. and the United States as to whether the question should be retained on the Council's agenda, which the former opposed and the latter favored. He made known his disagreement with the U.S. view, both in a memorandum to the President of the Security Council and by a personal intervention in the Council proceedings.

The Soviet Delegation supported his right to intervene, upon his own initiative as well as at the invitation of the Council. The U.S. Delegate, on the other hand, said he was "not at all sure that the Charter can be construed as authorizing the Secretary-General to make comments on political and substantive matters." The British Delegate at first inclined to the view that the members should "let experience show how

[9] G.A.O.R. (16th sess.), *Supplement 1A, Introduction to the Annual Report of the Secretary-General on the Work of the Organization, 16 June 1960-15 June 1961*, A/4800/Add. 1 (1961), p. 1.

the powers of the Secretary-General should be put into practice." Upon further reflection, he supported the Soviet view, as did the United States. Thereupon, the Security Council Rules of Procedure were revised, by unanimous consent, so as to permit the Secretary-General, or his deputy, to make written or oral statements to the Council "concerning any question under consideration by it." [10]

Intervention in a political dispute, so early in the Organization's history, involved an election on the part of the first Secretary-General to follow from the beginning a course calculated to develop the United Nations as an instrument for international cooperation, with an impartially functioning executive arm. Mr. Lie described his attitude in terms strikingly similar to those used some years later by Mr. Hammarskjold. Thus, in a letter to a friend, discussing the Iranian question, Mr. Lie said he had "tried to look at the matter as might a Foreign Minister of Norway confronted with a hypothetical case. . . ." [11] Mr. Hammarskjold, in his turn, said: "Often the Secretary-General has had to go into action where formerly a third government would have functioned, but where in this day and age, with present complex relations between governments, it has appeared simpler and more effective to turn to the Secretariat of the United Nations." [12] In fact, the history of the office, particularly since 1956, led him to refer, even more explicitly, to the "most controversial situations," in which "the Secretary-General was confronted with mandates of a highly general character, expressing the bare minimum of agreement attainable in the organs." [13] In such situations his objective was to apply the general principles of the Charter interpreted in the light of his honest judgment.

---

[10] The foregoing account, and quotations, are derived from Trygve Lie, *In the Cause of Peace: Seven Years with the United Nations* (New York: Macmillan, 1954), pp. 87-88.

[11] Same, p. 81.

[12] Address to Norwegian Association for the United Nations, University of Oslo, June 3, 1958. "Why the United Nations? An Answer," U.N., *Today's World and the United Nations: Four Addresses by Secretary-General Dag Hammarskjold* (New York: Author, 1958), pp. 25-26.

[13] Address at Oxford University (May 30, 1961), cited.

It would be too harsh a criticism to say that it is mere irresponsibility on the part of members to delegate such "highly general"—one might better say "hopelessly vague"— duties to the Secretary-General. The simple fact is, as he himself said, that "the serious problems arise precisely because it is so often not possible for the organs themselves to resolve the controversial issues faced by the Secretary-General." [14]

Thus, in 1956, at the time of the outbreak of hostilities in Egypt, he was asked "immediately to arrange with the parties concerned for the implementation of the cease-fire," and "to obtain compliance of the withdrawal of all forces behind the armistice lines." The same day, he was asked to submit a plan for setting up a United Nations Emergency Force.[15]

As if this were not a sufficient day's work, he was also requested by the Assembly to "investigate the situation caused by foreign intervention in Hungary . . . and as soon as possible to suggest methods to bring an end to the foreign intervention in Hungary in accordance with the principles of the Charter of the United Nations." [16] The remission of the question of Hungary to the United Nations in general, and to the Secretary-General in particular, and the tragically sterile consequences, exposed the Organization itself to bitter calumny. Yet, the fact is that the United States and other leading Western powers held back from taking, or suggesting, more specific measures. Hence, the Organization did no more, and no less, in the Hungarian case, than was asked of it by members.

In 1957 the General Assembly, declaring that Union of South Africa's policies of *apartheid* were inconsistent with the Charter, called upon it to "revise its policies," and requested the Secretary-General "to communicate with the Government of the Union of South Africa to carry forward the purposes of the present resolution." [17]

During the same month, the Assembly had turned its atten-

14 Same.
15 G.A. Resolutions 998 (ES I) and 999 (ES I), November 4, 1956.
16 G.A. Resolution 1004 (ES II), November 4, 1956.
17 G.A. Resolution 1016 (XI), January 30, 1957.

tion to the Middle East, and asked the Secretary-General "to continue his efforts for securing the complete withdrawal of Israel" from Egyptian territory.[18]

In 1958, again confronted with a crisis in the Middle East, the Assembly requested him "to make forthwith . . . such practical arrangements as would adequately help in upholding the purposes and principles of the Charter in relation to Lebanon and Jordan in the present circumstances. . . ."[19]

Interspersed with these highly controversial diplomatic assignments were requests, among many others, to make arrangements to clear the Suez Canal (Resolution 1121 [XI]); to make recommendations for strengthening and widening scientific activities in the field of atomic radiation studies (Resolution 1147 [XII]); to designate technical groups to study disarmament inspection measures (Resolution 1148 [XII]); to make urgent efforts to secure financing for the United Nations Relief and Works Agency for Palestine Refugees (Resolution 1191 [XII]); to recommend "steps that might be taken within the existing United Nations framework to encourage the fullest international co-operation for the peaceful uses of outer space" (Resolution 1348 [XIII]).

In addition to carrying out responsibilities in situations which had already exploded into crisis, the Secretary-General also engaged in what he called "active preventive diplomacy," where no government, or group of governments, or regional organization could take effective action. Thus, at the end of 1957, when Thailand and Cambodia turned to him for assistance in resolving a bitter dispute, he designated a conciliation commission which succeeded in effecting a settlement. In 1958 he sent a personal representative to Lebanon charged with responsibility, on his behalf, to carry out the ambiguous mission delegated to the Secretary-General in the Assembly Resolution of August 21, that of making "practical arrangements" to help uphold the Charter. The next year, he followed a similar procedure, entrusting to another representative the

---

[18] G.A. Resolution 1123 (XI), January 19, 1957.
[19] G.A. Resolution 1237 (ES III), August 21, 1958.

difficult task of conciliating factions struggling for power in Laos.

The concept of a "United Nations presence" had thus been forged—capable of pacifying, mediating, and in other ways injecting into a threatening situation the moderating influence of a nascent order.

The Secretary-General had not sought advance approval of the Security Council in any of these cases—an omission which brought from the Soviet government charges of usurpation of power. Nevertheless, the Secretary-General was always at pains to advise the political organs of his intention, to afford them opportunity for comment, and to render meticulous reports to them.

The hypocrisy of the Soviet attitude in this matter, as in its unwillingness to bear its share of the financial burdens of the U.N. and its rejection of the concept of an international civil service, is shown by the fact that on numerous occasions the Soviet government itself has supported resolutions charging the Secretary-General with vaguely phrased missions, which entrusted to him a wide scope for personal judgment. Notable examples may be found in the frequent Israel-Arab crises, the Suez affair, and the initial resolutions on the Congo.

It is not relevant to speculate how the office might have evolved under a different Secretary-General. The skill and wisdom which characterized Mr. Hammarskjold's actions are matters of wide acclaim. Nevertheless, it is not in the character of a democratic outlook to regard any man, however great, as irreplaceable. Shock and grief occasioned by Mr. Hammarskjold's untimely death led some normally astute friends and admirers to predict the end of the Organization.

The performance of his successors—and there will be many in the generations to come—will, of course, reflect their own qualities of judgment and character. But above all, the nature of their work and the function of their office will respond to the will and wisdom of the members, the United States in particular.

The late Secretary-General never reached for—nor did he shirk—the responsibilities implicit in the grant of controversial and ambiguous assignments. On occasion, however, he pointed out the risk to the Organization in playing what he called a "kind of lottery," in which members would seek to evade dilemmas by talking boldly and then remitting to the United Nations executive a general duty to work things out.

At a meeting with his Advisory Committee on the Congo early in 1961, he spoke of the necessity of keeping a negotiator "in a position to negotiate with those with whom he has to deal." He went on to say: "I have always considered that one of the classic examples of bad handling of a matter was the handling by the General Assembly of the China prisoner issue in the fall of 1954, when, in one and the same resolution, the General Assembly condemned Communist China and asked for negotiations with that country."

That mission, which he discharged with consummate skill, illuminates an aspect of the United Nations sometimes baffling to observers: its simultaneous use as a forum for recrimination and for reconciliation. The main reason for such apparently irrational behavior—which causes the traditional diplomatist to tear his hair—is that the United Nations in fact performs two quite inconsistent functions.

One is that of enabling members to give expression to their own national policies and purposes—often for domestic political effect. The other is to furnish a means for harmonizing action between nations.

The Secretariat is the best—and often the only—mechanism by which these incompatible uses can be adjusted. If the executive were itself transformed into an agency whose actions and decisions were subject to internal negotiation, it would become a mere committee of the parliamentary organ. This would have at least two adverse consequences.

One is that the so-called executive process would necessarily reflect and repeat the difficulties which had made it impossible for the parliamentary body to reach a clear-cut decision in the first place. Another is that the Secretariat would in essence be converted into a lower-level government representation, impeding impartial execution of decisions and likely to be enmeshed in controversies as to methods of implementing policies already laid down. Accordingly, the effect would be to prevent action when action is necessary. It is difficult to believe that the Soviet proposal for a triumvirate has any other purpose.

It has been said that a page of history is worth a volume of logic. Appraisal of a fully functioning United Nations executive may be aided by a glimpse behind the scenes of one or two significant moments of its history.

The first concerns negotiations between Mr. Hammarskjold and the government of Egypt concerning terms upon which the United Nations Emergency Force would take up its duties in Egypt.

In the face of the Israeli-British-French invasion in October 1956, the General Assembly held its First Emergency Special Session. Acting within the limits of its authority under the United Nations Charter, the Assembly on November 5, 1956, recommended the establishment of a United Nations Command for an emergency international force to secure and supervise the cessation of hostilities in Egypt, and requested the Secretary-General promptly to execute the resolution. The government of Egypt accepted this resolution in a telegram to the Secretary-General.

Next day, Mr. Hammarskjold submitted a report to the Assembly, suggesting principles to guide the functioning of such a force.[20] Prepared under extreme pressures of time, the report astutely balanced two countervailing legal and political issues: one, the right of the Assembly to determine the tasks of the force and the basis on which it must fulfill its mission; the other, the necessity for consent of the government of the territory on which the force would be stationed or operate. The report interpreted the function of the force to be to "help maintain quiet during and after the withdrawal of non-Egyptian troops, and to secure compliance with the other terms established in the resolution of 2 November, 1956." These terms, like all of the Suez resolutions, were vague and un-

20 "Second and Final Report . . . on the Plan for an Emergency International United Nations Force . . . ," G.A.O.R. (1st emer. spec. sess.), Annexes: Agenda Item 5, A/3302 (1956), pp. 19-26.

precise. As recommendations they were subject to acceptance by Egypt.

In the course of discussions with the commander of the force, General Burns, concerning implementation of the resolutions, the Egyptian government requested clarification as to how long it was contemplated the force would remain in Egypt.[21]

The Secretary-General responded that, while a definite reply was impossible, the emergency character of the force linked it to the liquidation of the crisis. Moreover, he said, if different views should arise as to the ending of the crisis, the question would have to be negotiated with the parties.

The Egyptian government persisted in seeking a more definite reply. In a memorandum dated November 11, 1956, the government noted that, since it was agreed that Egyptian consent was indispensable for entry and presence of the United Nations forces on its territory, "if such consent no longer persists, these forces shall withdraw."

The following day, November 12, the Secretary-General reminded Egypt that the conditions motivating its consent to entry and presence of the force were the same as those to which the General Assembly had directed the tasks of the force. Accordingly, he assumed it would be recognized that, so long as the task, thus prescribed, was not completed, the reasons for the consent of the government remain valid, hence withdrawal of consent prior to completion of the task would run counter to the acceptance by Egypt of the decision of the General Assembly. If a difference were to develop whether or not the reasons for the arrangements were still valid, the matter would be brought up for negotiation with the United Nations.

Immediately prior to the dispatch of this note, the Secretary-General and the government had agreed to publish their accord on entry of UNEF into Egypt. In view of previous exchanges, Mr. Hammarskjold did not anticipate that his note would introduce any new difficulty. Nevertheless, as he put it

[21] The following discussion is based upon authentic, though unpublished, sources.

some time later, he did recognize that there was an "element of gambling involved," which he felt he had to take, in view of the risks of further delay and the possibility that the Egyptian government might change its mind or seek even less satisfactory alternatives.

In fact, the next morning, November 13, Egypt advised the Secretary-General of its refusal to subscribe to his interpretation and insisted that the announced agreements remain inoperative until the misunderstanding was cleared up. This message caused a further delay of the transportation of troops to Egypt by at least twenty-four hours. The Secretary-General, in drafting a reply, felt it was now a "must" to get the troops in. He was confident that, in his own words, "I would be in a position to find a formula, saving the face of Egypt while protecting the U.N. stand, once I could discuss the matter personally with President Nasser."

The same day Mr. Hammarskjold sent messages to Egypt, making it clear that, if arrangements were permitted to break down over the principle that the troops must remain until completion of their task, he could "not avoid going to the General Assembly" for a decision as to what could or could not be accepted as an understanding.

Egypt thereupon permitted the troops to arrive, thus acquiescing in, although not expressly accepting, the Secretary-General's position.

In his effort to follow up the situation, in which different stands had been maintained by Egypt and himself, he was guided by the countervailing considerations reflected in his report of November 6, referred to earlier. On the one hand, Egypt had an undisputed constitutional right to request withdrawal of the troops, even though initial consent had been given. On the other hand, it now seemed possible, on the basis of Egypt's tacit acquiescence in his own stand, to induce that government to limit its freedom of action by agreeing to make a request for withdrawal of troops conditional upon the completion of their task. Whether or not the task was in fact completed would be a question which would have to be submitted to interpretation by the Assembly.

The Secretary-General decided to seek an agreement whereby Egypt would declare to the United Nations that it would exercise its full sovereign rights with regard to the troops on the basis of a "good faith interpretation" of the tasks of the force. The United Nations would make a reciprocal commitment to maintain the force so long as the task was not completed. Such a formula, while not explicitly providing for agreement between the United Nations and Egypt on withdrawal, came close to that line and preserved the principle upon which Mr. Hammarskjold had insisted. In effect, such an agreement would establish as a condition for withdrawal of the troops agreement upon the fact that their task was completed.

The Secretary-General proceeded to Capodachino, the UNEF staging area in Italy, and, during the night of November 15-16, elaborated a draft text along these lines.

During the evening and night of November 17, he met with President Nasser for seven hours, their discussion being limited virtually to this one issue. The President made clear to the Secretary-General he fully understood that, by limiting its freedom of action in this way, Egypt would take a serious step, since the question of the extent of the task would become decisive for the relations between Egypt and the United Nations and would determine Egypt's political freedom of action. The definition of the task in the Assembly resolutions was very loose; hence Egypt would be accepting a far-reaching and unpredictable restriction.

In the face of President Nasser's great reluctance, Mr. Hammarskjold felt obliged, in the course of the discussion, to threaten several times that, unless an agreement of this type was made, he would have to propose the immediate withdrawal of the troops.

An aide-mémoire embodying his point of view was in fact accepted by Egypt and reported to the General Assembly, which approved it without dissent on November 24, 1956.[22]

[22] G.A. (11th sess.), *Annex to Report of the Secretary-General on Basic Points for the Presence and Functioning in Egypt of the United Nations Emergency Force*, A/3375 (November 20, 1956); G.A. Resolution 1121 (XI).

In this situation, as in so many others, the Secretary-General was required to find a balance between the rights of national sovereignty and the legitimate concerns of the international community. This he was able to do through skillful exercise of all the attributes of a unified executive.

The Congo, too, involved all these, but with the added complexity of the Soviet bid for hegemony in Africa. From the beginning, the Secretary-General regarded his primary task as being to "counter efforts from all sides to make the Congo a happy hunting ground for national interests."

In late July and early August 1960, soon after the problem became critical, Mr. Hammarskjold concluded that he should propose to the General Assembly an arrangement for the whole of the civilian and military operation in the Congo, patterned after the United Nations Relief and Works Agency for Palestine. It was to have a Director-General and a small advisory committee, composed of states closely concerned. Because of the speed and pressure of events, however, he did not think it right to shift responsibility at that moment—and the moment never came.

There is a poignancy in the reasons he gave, some months prior to his death, for seeking such an arrangement: ". . . It has the advantage of not putting within the Secretariat tasks which, through their sheer mass, and also due to their quality, tend to swell like a kind of cancer and eat out all other necessary functions. The Congo operation has been and remains such a big burden on the Secretariat, one which encroaches very heavily on other tasks. . . . The idea has never died in my mind, and I would like to see it put into effect as soon as we get the situation under control."

As in the case of Suez, he subsequently established an advisory committee with which he conferred in private meetings at United Nations Headquarters. Shortly after the murder of Patrice Lumumba, the Security Council adopted a resolution urging "that the *United Nations* take immediately all appropriate measures to prevent the occurrence of civil war in the Congo . . ." as well as for the withdrawal and evacuation "of all Belgian and other foreign military and para-military personnel and political advisers not under the United Nations Command, and mercenaries." [23]

The phrase "United Nations" was used, rather than "Secretary-General," as a deliberate ambiguity, in order to avoid a veto by the Soviet Union, which had by then declared war on Mr. Hammarskjold. The ambiguity of the expression was compounded by another clause in the same resolution, reaffirming three earlier resolutions (all concurred in by the Soviets), which had explicitly assigned duties to the Secretary-General, and not to the "United Nations."

At the Security Council session the Soviet Delegate stated that "this resolution gives no mandate to the Secretary-General." However, he refused to explain what was meant by using the phrase the "United Nations" in a context calling for executive action. At the same session, the Secretary-General noted the reaffirmation of previous resolutions expressly entrusting his office with execution of the Security Council decisions in Congo affairs. He added: "On that basis I shall urgently avail myself of the valuable assistance of the Advisory Committee. It is from its members, fifteen of which are from African and Asian countries, that I will seek guidance in the implementation."

With this quiet challenge he carried forward, in defense of executive integrity, his historic duel with the Soviets begun a few months before by Mr. Khrushchev's sudden demand to have the office of Secretary-General replaced by a three-man executive, complete with the veto. He was, of course, aware that the Advisory Committee itself was divided and that the future of his office, as well as of the Congo, might well depend upon his capacity to lead the Committee to a consensus which would give vitality to the key resolution of February 21.

The Secretary-General met with his Advisory Committee on the afternoon of the same day the resolution was adopted by the Security Council. It was his twenty-third session with the Committee, and many more were to follow, but this was doubtless the most important one of all for the future of the operation.

[23] S.C. (942nd mtng.), S/4741 (February 21, 1961); author's italics.

Although this meeting, like all others, was private and hence the views expressed by members are entitled to privilege, the Secretary-General subsequently made available to others his own comments and reactions at the session.

In parliamentary manner, Mr. Hammarskjold proposed a "first reading" of the resolution, with a view to ironing out any differences of opinion. The first question he raised was the meaning of the term "United Nations," as used in the resolution. The Soviet contention that this did *not* refer to the Secretary-General left him free, if he wished, to disclaim any further responsibility. It was, therefore, necessary for him to insist upon a clear and definite outcome of the Committee consultations. If this were not possible, Mr. Hammarskjold saw no way to avoid going back to the Security Council for an interpretation.

By way of underscoring the executive tasks which the "United Nations" confronted under the resolution, he reminded the Committee of the conflicting groups in the Congo with which the Organization had to deal, and the controversial legal basis and aims of these dealings. From whom must consent be required; against whom could force be used? He referred to the Soviet contention that the Gizenga government was the legal government of the Congo, which implied that, although Gizenga could be dealt with only on the basis of consent, force might be used against others, including Kasavubu. Furthermore, Mr. Hammarskjold pointed out, the Security Council had not made it clear whether its resolution was governed by Article 40 of the Charter, merely contemplating recommendations to the parties, or by Article 42, under which it had power to use force, if necessary, to maintain peace and security. This question, in turn, bore on the stand of the governments contributing to the force, as well as on its activities in the Congo. Most of all, reinforcements were urgently needed.

Mr. Hammarskjold's forthright, yet tactful, posing of the issue of executive responsibility yielded its just fruits. After lengthy discussions, no one on the Committee openly dissented from the proposition that the phrase "United Nations," as

used in the resolution of February 21, meant, and could only
mean, the Secretary-General.

Throughout the session, Mr. Hammarskjold made it clear
that he was not seeking to unburden himself of his responsibilities. He sought advice, not decisions. He commented: "It
has been said, in what I am afraid is the usual sentimental
spirit of friends in the Press, that the Secretary-General has
the most lonely job in the world. Let us use more professional
language, and let us say that he is very badly off in enlightened advice. So that it is always a question of finding the best
form in which he can get such advice. . . ."

When all who wished had spoken, he summed up concisely:
". . . If I act on the assumption that this resolution must be
considered as putting the responsibility for implementation
on the Secretary-General in forms established for the Congo
operation, I would act in accordance with the principles held
by those I have had the honor and privilege to consult."

To this there was no dissent. The Soviet position had been
rejected through parliamentary processes, led by persuasion
and firmness. From that moment on, no member doubted
where executive responsibility for United Nations action in
the Congo resided, though of course some exercised to the full
their right to question interpretations of a resolution whose
very ambiguity was a device of their own choosing.

The prerequisites for an effectively functioning executive
were expressed by Alexander Hamilton in a four-word summary: "Decision, activity, secrecy and despatch." [24] Mr. Hammarskjold applied these qualities with skill and vigor, though
perhaps he might have preferred the phrase "quiet diplomacy"
to "secrecy."

His continual search for "enlightened advice" was to help
make a wise decision, but never to delay reaching a decision.
The danger lurking in a formula requiring consultation with
a council of subordinates, as a condition of action—if not,
indeed, of office—was given expression, again by Hamilton, in
the same *Federalist* paper. He warned that executive unity

24 *The Federalist*, no. 70.

may be destroyed: ". . . by vesting it ostensibly in one man, subject, in whole or in part, to the control and cooperation of others, in the capacity of counsellors to him. . . . A council to a magistrate, who is himself responsible for what he does, are generally nothing better than a clog upon his good intentions, are often the instruments and accomplices of his bad, and are almost always a cloak to his faults."

When the question of appointing a Secretary-General arises again in the General Assembly, as it inevitably will, in the fall of 1962, heed should be paid to the wisdom of our own founding fathers, amply confirmed by the experience of our republic. Expedients which may be contrived as concessions to Soviet obstinacy exact too high a price if they deform the slowly evolving structure of peace.

Chapter II

The Security Council— as Enforcer of the Peace

The Security Council was designed as the muscle to enforce the Charter. It early became muscle-bound.

The reservation of the veto to the five permanent members, as a condition upon performance of the role assigned to the Council, was intended to assure that no collective action could be taken without the consent of each. Subordination of the Council's primary responsibility to the rule of unanimity foreclosed from the beginning the dependability of the Council as an agency to enforce peace.

Insistence upon so special a privilege was explained in only vague and complex terms. Perhaps the most plausible explanation is that embodied in a joint statement of the sponsoring powers, at San Francisco: "In view of the primary responsibilities of the permanent members, they could not be expected, in the present condition of the world, to assume the obligation to act in so serious a matter as the maintenance of international peace and security in consequence of a decision in which they had not concurred." [1]

To many of the smaller nations, this statement had a hollow ring. The "condition of the world" in fact seemed to make it all the more necessary for the permanent members to assume such an obligation, precisely because of their primary responsibilities.

[1] *Documents of the United Nations Conference on International Organization, San Francisco, 1945*, v. 11: *Commission III: Security Council* (London and New York: U.N. Information Organizations, 1945), p. 713.

It was generally perceived that enforcement action against a great power risked major war. Nevertheless, concern about becoming involved in a major war is not a function of size; every nation at San Francisco was engaged in one at that very moment. Many of them believed it was a war which might have been averted if the great powers had exercised, rather than hedged, their primary responsibilities.

It remains true, nevertheless, that no great power would have been—or is today—willing to bind itself in advance to compulsory process for collective action. This is a political fact of life. Whether or not it is a meritorious position is an academic question.

The Veto: Rationale and Reality

The basic motivations for insistence upon the veto power were in major respects peculiar to each of the several nations concerned.

Thus, Soviet demand for the special privilege undoubtedly reflected the nature of the Soviet system itself which, as has been said, "can offer no plan for a stable world order that is not an extension of its own sphere of power—that is not, in fact, a hegemony." [2] The Soviets have acted true to form, using the veto power in issues far removed from the "maintenance of international peace and security," and in violation of the promise made at San Francisco, along with the other great powers, not to "use their 'veto' power wilfully to obstruct the operation of the Council." The Soviet Delegation has blocked more than ninety Council resolutions by its negative vote. These include such proposals as keeping the Spanish question on the agenda in 1946; establishment of a commission to investigate border incidents in the Balkans; approval of the U.N. Atomic Energy Commission's plan for atomic control, as well as numerous other disarmament proposals; a request that the Commission for Indonesia continue its work; the appointment of either Trygve Lie or Lester B. Pearson as Secretary-

[2] The phrase is that of François Bondy, editor of *Preuves*.

General; and, of course, a large number of resolutions for the admission of new members.

Reckless Soviet abuse of the veto should not, however, be allowed to obscure the truth that the other great powers were equally insistent upon the same right. The British and French had their own reasons for demanding special privilege as great powers. These were—and remain—largely connected with the maintenance of sovereignty over colonial empire. The concept of hegemony was latent also in Sir Winston Churchill's plan for a "Supreme World Council," in which the great powers would preside over subordinate regional councils.

As for the United States, our motives were both mixed and inconsistent. The American people and leaders realized that the privilege reserved by the Big Five offered a challenge to responsibility as well as a device for power. Franklin Roosevelt spoke of a special role for the "Four Policemen," presumably without forgetting the traditional lot of the policeman. Secretary of State Stettinius, in his Report to the President, said that "peace is a world-wide problem and the *maintenance* of peace, and not merely its *restoration,* depends primarily upon the unity of the great powers." [3] Both leaders reflected the American experience that the evil lies not so much in the reservation of power as in its abuse, and that man has never yet devised an alternative to self-discipline.

Prior to the San Francisco Conference the great powers had agreed at Dumbarton Oaks upon the requirement of unanimity with respect to enforcement action by the Council. Subsequently, at the Crimea Conference in February 1945, Marshal Stalin reluctantly accepted President Roosevelt's proposal that, though unanimity would apply to Council action regarding pacific settlement of disputes (Chapter VI of the Charter), members which are parties to disputes must abstain from Council decisions relating thereto (Article 27[3]).

At San Francisco, the United States fought a winning battle

[3] "Report to the President on the Results of the San Francisco Conference" (June 26, 1945), in *The Charter of the United Nations,* Hearings before the Senate Committee on Foreign Relations, 79th Cong., 1st sess., July 9-13, 1945 (Washington: GPO, 1945; rev.), p. 72.

against Soviet insistence upon the application of the veto to block consideration or discussion by the Council of a dispute or situation. At the same time, American insistence upon the veto with respect to substantive decisions of the Council remained firm and unyielding. At one point during the conference, when several delegations of smaller nations became somewhat unruly in their opposition to the veto, Senator Tom Connally felt it expedient to reprimand them. "You may go home from San Francisco—if you wish," he said sternly, "and report that you have defeated the veto. . . . But you can also say, 'We tore up the Charter!'" [4]

The Senate of the United States made clear the importance it attached to the veto, stressing in its report on the Charter that "no enforcement action of any kind against a nation breaking the peace can be taken, without the full concurrence of the United States acting through its delegate on the Security Council." And in 1956, a Senate subcommittee reaffirmed this view of the Senate, expressing its belief "that the veto power should be retained unimpaired," except in the cases of pacific settlement and the admission of new members. There is little reason to think that U.S. policy—any more than that of any other great power—will undergo a material change in this respect in the foreseeable future.

The contrast between the Soviet and U.S. attitudes toward the meaning of "great-power unity" and the abuse of power was brought out clearly during the 1950 debates on the Uniting for Peace Resolution.[5] The Soviet Delegate, Mr. Vishinsky, attacked the proposal to enable the General Assembly to carry out its responsibilities in the maintenance of peace and security, on the ground that unanimity is the "cornerstone" and "foundation" of the United Nations, hence the proposals "would explode and crush the Charter."

This was, of course, a distortion of the true significance of the requirement of unanimity, treating the veto as if it were

[4] Quoted in Francis O. Wilcox and Carl M. Marcy, *Proposals for Changes in the United Nations* (Washington: Brookings Institution, 1955), p. 311.

[5] G.A. Resolution 377 (V), November 3, 1950, by which the General Assembly is enabled to act quickly in the event the Security Council is precluded from carrying out its peace-keeping function because of a veto.

a device of power, rather than of responsibility. It was a pointed admission of Soviet belief in power for its own sake. It was an example of that twisted attribute of the Communist doctrine, which leaves logic dangling at the end of a rope too short to reach the truth.

In sponsoring the Uniting for Peace Resolution, the United States took fully into account the primary responsibility of the Security Council "to ensure prompt and effective action" for maintaining peace and security (Article 24 [1]). The resolution does not pre-empt that responsibility. It merely erects safeguards against the consequences of inaction.

It is commonplace, and quite accurate, to say that the veto is not a disease so much as a symptom of international anemia. The smaller powers at San Francisco expressed attitudes toward the veto which are helpful in appraising chances of marshaling support for the much discussed "liberalization of voting procedures," including abolition of the veto power.

Many of them, particularly some among the American republics, did not criticize the veto in principle. They resented the big-power monopoly, and spoke nostalgically of the Council of the League of Nations, where all states there represented, both large and small, had the veto. Another group were sufficiently confident of their relations with one or another great power so as to feel no concern about the denial of the right to themselves. Still others, notably certain neighbors of the Soviet Union, feared the consequences to themselves of any action taken without unanimity, hence they endorsed the veto as a safeguard against being caught in the center of a conflict among the giants. Moreover, those states which attacked the principle of the veto found it impossible to agree upon alternative procedures.

After all, unanimity is the traditional rule for international conferences. Majority rule developed chiefly in international organizations of a technical character. Unanimity is still the rule in even such congenial groupings as NATO and the Organization for Economic Cooperation and Development. The small members tend to regard the veto as a defense against dictation; the larger, a shield against irresponsible majorities.

The significant advance in the United Nations is acceptance by the great powers—at least in principle—of majority decisions in numerous situations.

It would manifestly be absurd to contend that voting procedures in a parliamentary organ are without practical consequence. It requires rare qualities of character to reach consensus in the silent manner of the Friends. Nevertheless, too close scrutiny of the *means* of voting often tends to produce myopia concerning the *ends* of voting.

Further assessment of this matter will be relevant to the consideration below (p. 73) of proposals for "weighted voting" in the General Assembly and of other parliamentary practices suggested as a means to give ballast to responsibility. As to such devices, the United States has often emphasized—as it should continue to do—that although structure is important, nevertheless the "problems today presented to those who desire peace are not questions of structure. . . . They require performances of obligations already undertaken, fidelity to pledges already given." [6]

Apart from the functions assigned to the Security Council by Chapter VI of the Charter with regard to the pacific settlement of disputes,[7] the preoccupation of the Charter is to vest power in the Council to take action, by force if necessary, for the maintenance of peace.

There is a tendency to attribute to the Security Council a

[6] Testimony of Secretary of State George C. Marshall (May 5, 1948), *Structure of the United Nations and the Relations of the United States to the United Nations,* Hearings before the House Committee on Foreign Affairs, 80th Cong., 2d sess., May 4-14, 1948 (Washington: GPO, 1948), p. 43.

[7] For the sake of completeness, mention should be made of other functions relating to peace and security, such as: formulation of plans for the regulation of armaments (Article 26); initiatives to procure agreements making armed forces available (Article 43); determination of strength and readiness of air force contingents, if any, available for enforcement action (Article 45); plans for the application of armed force (Article 46); exercise of United Nations functions relating to strategic trusteeships (Article 83). The *Supplements* to the *Repertoire of the Practice of the Security Council* (ST/PSCA/1) prepared by the United Nations, reveal that since 1952 the Council has taken no decision in the exercise of any of these functions and powers.

corporate personality far beyond its means. The great powers are not members of the Security Council because it has the primary function of maintaining peace; the Council has this primary function because they are members. The Security Council is a vehicle of power because it comprises the engines of power. Abuse of power by those who hold primary responsibilities has deprived the Security Council of the possibility of serving as a dependable agency to enforce peace. Instead, it has become an arena of conflicting interests and attitudes.

It would, nevertheless, be a mistake for the United States to "write off" the Security Council. Because of its constitutional role, small size and—with the exception of the veto— its flexible processes, the Council remains a convenient forum for maneuver in crisis. That it should be available for this purpose was the prudent intent of Article 28, enjoining the Council "to be so organized as to be able to function continuously." It is of vital importance, politically, if not strategically, for the smaller powers to have recourse to a forum whose door is always open.

Thus, in 1950, Ecuador, disregarding strenuous objections on the part of the United States, persisted in sponsoring a Security Council invitation to representatives of the Chinese Communist government to attend meetings of the Council during discussion of Chinese charges of U.S. aggression against Taiwan.[8] The informal, and patently sincere, explanation given by the Ecuadoran Ambassador to our delegation was that his country, like other small American republics, regarded it as a matter of national security that a forum be provided for any charge of aggression, however ill-founded or malicious.

The availability of a suitable forum is normally of at least as much concern as the precise nature of the forum. This

---

[8] S.C., *Ecuador: Proposal Reintroduced in the Security Council . . . Complaint of Armed Invasion of Taiwan*, S/1823/Corr. 1 (September 29, 1950). The ensuing sessions provide a case study of vituperation and a grim foretaste of the Chinese Communist behavior if they were to gain a seat in the Council.

raises the question of relative priority, if any, to be given regional arrangements as against more universal groupings. Chapter VIII of the Charter not only envisages the existence of regional arrangements but exhorts their members to try to settle disputes through such arrangements "before referring them to the Security Council." [9]

Peace-Keeping by Regions

Frustration of hopes that the United Nations would serve as an instrument adequate to keep the peace has spurred an anxious quest for alternatives. Some call for drastic overhaul of the United Nations; others involve allotropic forms of world government. The former would require amendment of the Charter, which could be vetoed by the very states whose conduct makes the amendments desirable. The latter are, for the most part, blueprints of a vision.

By 1948, public debate had begun to center largely upon the project for a mutual defense arrangement between the United States and certain European nations, which was to ripen into the North Atlantic Treaty in the spring of 1949. The strongest impetus to the formation of NATO came from the alarming trend of events in Europe. But the search for new security arrangements reflected also a widespread agreement that the peace-keeping functions of the United Nations had been thwarted by the intransigence of the Soviet Union, made manifest through abuse of the veto and other forms of obstructive conduct. The Security Council was veto-bound. Defense of the Charter required building new ramparts.

There was inevitable disagreement concerning the role of regional or other defense pacts, as distinguished from procedures which could be devised inside the United Nations but

[9] Article 52(2). The article was invoked to justify the Council's denial of the request by Guatemala in 1954 to take up its complaint of aggression by Honduras and Nicaragua. The then government of Guatemala had succeeded in blocking consideration of the question by the Organization of American States, favoring the more congenial environment of the United Nations, that is to say, the presence of the Soviet Union. (S.C.O.R. [675th mtng.], S/PV.675 [1954], para. 60.)

outside the veto, to paraphrase a comment of the late Senator Vandenberg.

A project which gained some favor as early as 1948 envisaged a pact or protocol by which members of the United Nations would voluntarily bind themselves to come to the aid of a victim of aggression if requested to do so by a specified vote in the General Assembly or the Security Council.[10]

The Uniting for Peace Resolution, discussed below, goes part of the way in this direction, but with the crucial difference that the General Assembly is limited to making recommendations, hence members are not precommitted to join in collective enforcement action.

Warnings were sounded, echoes of which still reverberate, against disuniting the nations that could act effectively for peace and weakening the world organization through excessive emphasis on regionalism. It was pointed out "that nations which are included in a regional scheme will tend to feel that it sets the practical limits of their obligations; and that those not included will drift gradually into another camp." [11]

In other words, the dilemma of regionalism inheres in all plans to coalesce the parts without fragmenting the whole. Such fragmentation involves strategic as well as political hazards, particularly to nations like the United States with world-wide interests which defy efforts to draw chalk lines of responsibility or commitments on the map. On the other hand, the United States found in the ensuing years that it was faced with specific threats in specific areas, and sought to meet them primarily by extending into the Middle East and the Far East its regional alliance system, which seemed to give promise of the immediate and effective action likely to be needed.

By mid-1955, the Joint Chiefs of Staff were split by divergent views regarding the extent of our bilateral and regional commitments, as well as our capacity to meet them.

10 Such an agreement, it was argued, was permissible within the meaning of Article 51 of the Charter, preserving the "right of individual or *collective* self-defense. . . ." See, for example, Hamilton Fish Armstrong, "Coalition for Peace," *Foreign Affairs*, October 1948.

11 Hamilton Fish Armstrong, "Regional Pacts: Strong Points or Storm Cellars?" *Foreign Affairs*, April 1949, p. 361.

The War Department leaked to the press a memorandum of General Matthew Ridgway, in which the General complained of U.S. commitments, "some vague, some specific, to take action, to deploy forces, and to provide material support" to: Canada, twenty Latin American republics, Berlin, West Germany, Spain, Yugoslavia, eleven North Atlantic Treaty nations, Libya, Ethiopia, Saudi Arabia, Iran, Australia, New Zealand, Pakistan, Philippines, Korea, Japan, and the Republic of China.[12]

However, there seemed no practical alternative to such arrangements and commitments—not as substitutes for the United Nations, but as military bulwarks of the Charter. That had already become clear, with respect to Europe, in the latter 1940s. Thus, in its unanimous report on the North Atlantic Treaty, the Senate Foreign Relations Committee emphasized that the treaty was ". . . designed to strengthen the system of law based on the purposes and principles of the United Nations. It should go far to remove any uncertainty which might mislead potential aggressors as to the determination of the parties fully to carry out their obligations under the Charter and collectively to resist an armed attack." [13]

The importance of the North Atlantic Treaty Organization to the defense of the United States, Europe and the free world justifies close attention to the practical possibilities of enlarging its political and economic base, as contemplated by Articles 2 and 4 of the treaty. NATO and the United Nations are designed to serve mutually supporting, rather than contradictory, purposes. The Charter of the United Nations, as a declaration of common purposes, embodies fundamental principles to which the NATO partners are dedicated, although in varying degrees of practical application.

Nevertheless, as the Committee of Three Foreign Ministers pointed out in their 1956 report: "North Atlantic political and economic cooperation, however, let alone unity, will not

---

[12] *The New York Times,* July 15, 1955.
[13] *North Atlantic Treaty,* Executive Report no. 8 of the Senate Committee on Foreign Relations, 81st Cong., 1st sess. (Washington: GPO, 1949), p. 7.

be brought about in a day or by a declaration, but by creating over the years and through a whole series of national acts and policies, the habits and traditions and precedents for such co-operation and unity." [14]

This is in essence, also, the premise underlying suggestions such as that of Senator Fulbright, to "develop a full-fledged community" of the Atlantic nations and—looking beyond the frontiers of the Western world—for a world-wide "concert of free nations." [15]

This appeal recognizes the "slow and painful trend toward unification." It expresses a realistic awareness that the difficulties do not stem from lack of available procedures for cooperation. On the contrary, the approach concedes that the trouble with the machinery "in NATO, in O.E.C.D., in the U.N. and elsewhere. . . . is that it is not used and the reason that it is not used is the absence of a conscious sense of community among the free nations."

The development of such a sense of community, through concrete and often politically unpopular programs, would endow all these agencies with greater peace-keeping as well as peace-building capacity. They would then be truly complementary and mutually supporting. A sense of community, or common interest, is the essential precondition of even the most rudimentary "concert of free nations," however broadly or narrowly that term may be conceived.

It may fairly be said, perhaps, that just as designs for world government are unattainable and even diversionary, so projects for supranational institutions on a NATO-wide basis often ignore the vast geographical expanse of NATO itself, which, for valid defense reasons, spans many seas and several

[14] The three "Wise Men" were Lester B. Pearson of Canada, Halvard Lange of Norway, and Gaetano Martino of Italy. They concluded that there was need for closer political consultation, but that there were no "significant new areas for collective economic action requiring execution by NATO itself." (*Report of the Committee of Three on Non-Military Co-operation in NATO*, U.S. Department of State Publication no. 6449, International Organization and Conference Series, I, 32 [Washington: GPO, 1957].)

[15] J. W. Fulbright, "For a Concert of Free Nations," *Foreign Affairs*, October 1961, p. 15 ff.

continents. Moreover, many problems besetting its members have roots in all parts of the world and deeply affect the destiny of nations which, though far removed from the NATO area, may be closely linked in outlook and purpose with North Atlantic nations.

SEATO and CENTO likewise provide a useful framework for defense assistance and coordination. Nevertheless, those organizations, unlike NATO, have not aroused wide popular response in the areas of their operation, and have failed to take root in political, economic or cultural soil.[16]

It is significant, also, that parties to regional arrangements, other than the Organization of American States, do not tend to use such arrangements for settlement of their own disputes. Even the history of NATO in this respect demonstrates that what counts in resolving disputes is not so much the choice of a forum as a genuine desire to settle, which always carries with it a willingness to lose. Britain was no more willing to submit the Cyprus question to NATO than to the United Nations. France has revealed no eagerness to seek NATO's mediation in the Algerian crisis, even though the North Atlantic Treaty includes "the Algerian departments of France" within the area of the treaty's protection (Article 6). Likewise, the Suez dispute involved open and bitter disagreement among NATO partners, but was not discussed within the Treaty Organization.

Hence the evidence suggests that disputes submitted to international processes are more likely to visit the United Nations than regional bodies. The priority for the latter, envisaged by Article 52(2), has not materialized, execpt in the inter-American community where the Organization of Ameri-

---

16 Thus, Asoka Mehta, an anti-Communist Indian leader, has commented: ". . . unlike the NATO countries, the policy of military alliance with the West has brought little understanding between the governments and people in most of the CENTO and SEATO countries in Asia. The exceptions like South Korea, Taiwan, South Viet-Nam, and the Philippines are due more to local considerations than to global reasons." ("An Asian Perspective on Peace," speech at Carnegie Endowment for International Peace, July 7, 1960, in *Report on the Fiftieth Anniversary of the Carnegie Endowment for International Peace* [New York: Author, 1961], p. 30.)

can States has been able to work out effective processes for handling most disputes among its members as a vital element in the hemispheric system of security and cooperation.

Future Role of the Security Council

Discussion of the Security Council thus far has related primarily to its stated purposes and formal processes. However, as the late Secretary-General Hammarskjold reminded us, continuous opportunities for talks among its members have "enabled it to exert its influence during the intervals when it does not meet in public." [17] Such informal discussions aid in forming consensus, in identifying areas of agreement and disagreement, and in exerting diplomatic pressures, without publicity, in support of settlement of protracted or smoldering controversies. Furthermore the Secretary-General, by means of private discussions with Council members, may receive helpful guidance in carrying out Council resolutions which delegate to him vaguely defined responsibilities.

Many new tasks devolve upon a state when it is elected to a nonpermanent seat on the Council. It assumes a tacit, yet perceptible, duty toward all states with which it may be grouped by geography or tradition. These expect their views to be heeded, or at least understood, by their colleague on the Council. When differences arise within the group or area, the delegation often finds itself in a cross fire. It has a corresponding opportunity to mediate and to persuade.

In the course of such efforts, influence can be exerted by delegates to the Security Council in at least two directions: upon each other and upon their home governments. Accord-

[17] G.A.O.R. (14th sess.), *Supplement 1A, Introduction to the Annual Report of the Secretary-General on the Work of the Organization, 16 June 1958-15 June 1959*, A/4132/Add. 1 (1959), p. 3. Inferences as to the "decline of the Council," based merely upon frequency of its meetings, are misleading. During its first five years, the Council met 528 times, as against only 178 meetings in its second five years. The sparse five meetings of 1959 seemed to signal the end of the Council as a functioning body. Then came the Congo, and the Council met more often in 1960 than in any year since 1948.

ingly, the United States has a high interest in encouraging member nations to designate representatives of high caliber and to offer all practicable assistance to their delegations.

We do well, also, in supporting efforts to enlarge the Council, to take account of the doubled membership of the Organization. The Asian and African states are not adequately represented, and it would appear appropriate to add at least two new seats. This, however, requires amendment of the Charter and the Soviet Union continues to threaten to veto any such amendment until the Chinese representation question is "solved."

Standards for deciding which candidates for Council membership the United States will support, as well as our tactics once we have made a decision, are erratic. A practice has arisen of acquiescing in the majority choice of regional caucuses, thus often committing U.S. support and prestige to candidates of dubious quality. This practice, moreover, encourages political trading within the caucuses, so that Member A supports Member B this year for reciprocal favors next year, and the like.

The salutary process of voting for members by secret ballot, called for by the Rules of Procedure, has long since become merely nominal. Worst of all, not even lip service is paid any longer to the Charter injunction to pay due regard, in election of members, to their contribution "to the maintenance of international peace and security" (Article 23, para. 1). The organ cannot command respect if the methods of composing it are degraded. The United States has joined in a general carelessness on this matter. It is time for improvement.

In sum, the Security Council—though undependable as an agency to enforce the Charter—fulfills an important role as an organ of consultation and of diplomatic maneuver. It would be wrong to say that, because the enforcement muscle is cramped, the organ as a whole is atrophied. And it would be even more rash to predict that a time will never come again, as in the early days of the Congo crisis, when the right of urgent recourse to the Security Council could avert immediately threatened disaster.

Major shifts of policy of the great powers are as likely to show up first in the Security Council as anywhere else. It remains, like the General Assembly, a forum of self-revelation and this, even in international affairs, is the beginning of wisdom.

Chapter III

The General Assembly— as Keeper of the Peace

Within a year after the General Assembly had begun functioning, it became clear that its responsibilities for keeping peace had outrun its procedures. In the fall of 1947, the United States sponsored a proposal that the Assembly establish an Interim Committee, which would be available between sessions for the purpose of studying matters committed to it at a prior session or slated for inclusion on the agenda of a subsequent one.

In a statement explaining the proposal, the U.S. Delegation, through Mr. Dulles, outlined the General Assembly's "vast range of responsibilities." The statement stressed in particular its "great authority in relation to the maintenance of international peace and security," describing that authority as "partly exclusive, partly parallel, partly residual." [1]

The reference to the "residual" character of the Assembly's responsibilities for peace helps put into perspective what is often erroneously described as an unwarranted shift of power from the Security Council to the Assembly. Soviet leaders, in particular, have challenged the Assembly's discharge of peace-keeping responsibilities as a corruption of the Charter.

[1] Statement by John Foster Dulles before First Committee of the General Assembly (October 14, 1947), G.A.O.R. (2d sess.), *First Committee: Political and Security Questions . . . Summary Record of Meetings, 16 September-19 November 1947* (1947), p. 130. The central source of the Assembly's power is, of course, Article 10, authorizing it to recommend to members, or to the Security Council, with respect to "any matters within the scope of the present Charter."

True to Communist notions of hegemony, the Soviets have opposed efforts to tailor the Assembly's procedures to match its broad duties in the maintenance of peace. Their attack upon the constitutionality of the 1947 proposal to set up the Interim Committee, and their subsequent boycott of the Committee's work, was one of the first clear signals of the cold war. It coincided with the termination of efforts to reach agreement with respect to the organization of armed forces to be made available to the Council under Article 43 of the Charter.[2] Outside the United Nations, the Soviet government was, during the same period, instructing its Eastern European client states to reject the United Kingdom-French bid to participate in a joint European-wide recovery program.

The Soviet government is, however, not the only one to look askance at projects to equip the General Assembly with means enabling it to do its business. The leader of the French government, President Charles de Gaulle, voicing concern regarding the Assembly's "tumultuous and scandalous meetings," has expressed the view that the General Assembly should be limited to debating only questions submitted to it by the Security Council.[3]

Some, fearful that the increase in Assembly membership inflates the risks of irresponsibility, talk wistfully of the "good old days" when the United States was confident of marshaling majority sentiment in the Council, even if Soviet vetoes precluded action to give effect to the sentiment.[4] It is fair to say that such retrospection involves a flight from the facts of

[2] The last discussion of this matter by the Council was at its 157th meeting, July 15, 1947.

[3] *The New York Times,* April 12, 1961.

[4] Thus, it is reported by Thomas J. Hamilton, Chief of the United Nations Bureau of *The New York Times* (though without citing evidence): ". . . the outlook in the Assembly is so dark that the Western powers are now in a mood to go back to the Security Council. There, for the time being at least, they have the needed 7 out of 11 votes." ("U.S. and Changed UN," *The United Nations in Crisis,* Headline Series no. 149 [New York: Foreign Policy Association-World Affairs Center, 1961], p. 30.) It is far from clear what "going back" to the Council means. No major issue has been brought before the Council by any great power since June 25, 1950, except for Suez and Hungary in 1956, and these were before the Council en route to the Assembly.

power rather than a studied advance toward more effective uses of power and influence in the United Nations.

Mr. Dulles' reference in 1947 to the "residual" authority of the General Assembly in relation to maintaining peace and security rests on sound Charter doctrine and unassailable logic. Notwithstanding Soviet insistence that the Charter confers *exclusive* powers on the Security Council—a conclusion implicit in the twisted significance Soviet spokesmen give to the concept of "great-power unity"—the Charter in fact merely endows the Council with *"primary* responsibility for the maintenance of international peace and security" (Article 24[1]). Moreover, the Charter authorizes members to bring any dispute, or any situation which might lead to friction, "to the attention of the Security Council *or* of the General Assembly" (Article 35).

The members of the United Nations did not delegate to the Council primary responsibility for their survival as a gesture of courtesy. If the leaders of nations had willfully left a mere vacuum in the event of the Council's failure to discharge its primary responsibility, they would have betrayed the vital interests of their peoples. As Mr. Dulles told the Senate Committee on Foreign Relations in 1945: "The small powers at San Francisco were not afraid that the Security Council would act; their only fear was that it would not act." [5]

Korea

The deliberate, though vaguely formulated, distribution of power between the Security Council and the General Assembly was designed to minimize the risk of such a vacuum. Korea furnished striking evidence of the realism of the formula.

Soviet absence from the Security Council on June 25, 1950, is often cited as an "accident" or "error," which alone made

[5] Statement of John Foster Dulles (July 13, 1945), *The Charter of the United Nations,* Hearings before the Senate Committee on Foreign Relations, 79th Cong., 1st sess., July 9-13, 1945 (Washington: GPO, 1945; rev.), p. 643.

possible adoption of a resolution from which all subsequent United Nations action in Korea stemmed. In fact, that occasion marked the fourth abortive Soviet attempt to preclude Council action by voluntary absence from its sessions.[6]

Accordingly, when Communist aggression was launched against the Republic of Korea, the "common law" of the Charter on this matter was sufficiently accepted so that no delegation raised a question at the session of June 25 concerning the Council's competence to act, notwithstanding Soviet absence from the meeting. Moreover, consideration had been given by the U.S. government to the possibility that the Soviet Delegate might show up at the session for the purpose of exercising a veto. The U.S. Delegation had therefore prepared to request Secretary-General Lie to summon a special session of the Assembly the following day. Such a meeting would have taken place if—as was virtually certain under the circumstances—a majority of the members concurred in the request.[7]

Resolutions by the General Assembly relating to Korea would have had no more, or less, compulsive legal effect than the several Security Council resolutions which were adopted on Korea on June 25, 1950, and thereafter. These were all based upon the power of the Council under Chapter VI of the Charter to recommend methods for settling disputes, and were not legally binding decisions.

The return of the Soviet Delegate to the Security Council on August 1, 1950, reduced it to impotence so far as further action on Korea was concerned. Except for a few strident and unproductive Council sessions, all future United Nations action regarding Korea centered in the General Assembly, act-

---

[6] Three earlier attempts were rebuffed by the Council: in the Iranian case (1946, 30th meeting; S.C., *Letter from . . . Gromyko to the President of the Security Council . . .* , S/30 (April 6, 1946); in the question of disarmament (1950, 462d meeting); and in the Kashmir case (1950, 471st meeting).

[7] General Assembly Rules of Procedure, Rule 9. The Rules were later amended in the Uniting for Peace Resolution so as to permit any seven members of the Security Council, as well as a majority of the members of the Organization, to request an emergency special session of the Assembly.

ing under its "residual" power to maintain or restore peace. Indeed, in January 1951, the Security Council formally removed the Korean item from its agenda, thereby acknowledging a state of sterility which had actually existed since the preceding August.

The Assembly went on to take such important actions as condemning Communist China as an aggressor in Korea (February 1, 1951) and calling for an embargo on shipments of strategic items to areas under its control (May 18, 1951). Moreover, all activities relating to the armistice took place under the Assembly's supervision.

It may be useful, in appraising the mutually supporting roles of the Security Council and the General Assembly in the Korean case, to recall the purpose of the United Nations military action in that country. It had one principal objective: to repel North Korean—and subsequently Chinese—aggression against the Republic of Korea.

The United States' political objective with respect to Korea, prior to the Communist aggression, had reflected General Assembly resolutions which called for the establishment, by peaceful means, of a unified, independent and democratic nation. This end, of course, remained the hope of the United States, even after the North Korean and Chinese aggression. However, the United States had never undertaken to accomplish that objective by force, and the Communist attack upon the Republic of Korea did not impose such a commitment upon us, although obviously the desired result would have been attained had it been practicable to eliminate the forces of aggression from all of Korea.

Criticisms of the United Nations action in Korea often reflect misconception as to the facts. It is sometimes said that the United Nations inhibited the United States' freedom of maneuver; in particular, that Chinese air power was permitted sanctuary beyond the Yalu River. In fact, the conduct of military operations was at all times under U.S. direction; limitations upon military action in Korea were self-imposed and dictated by over-all strategic considerations.

Consultations were frequently held with a committee composed of representatives of the fifteen nations which contributed to combat services in Korea. Those nations, however, recognized the dominant responsibility of the United States in exercising the Unified Command, particularly in the light of the overwhelming share of the burden borne throughout by the United States.

Another criticism sometimes voiced is that the United Nations became "judge in its own cause" by becoming a "party to the dispute," and that its effectiveness as a mediatory agency was thereby impaired. Such criticism misconceives both the nature of the conflict and of the United Nations itself. Communist aggression in Korea was much more than a phase of a bipolar power struggle. As was made clear at the outset, in the first statement by the U.S. Delegation to the Security Council on June 25, 1950: "A full-scale attack is now going forward in Korea. . . . It is armed aggression against the Government elected under United Nations supervision. Such an attack strikes at the fundamental purposes of the United Nations Charter. Such an attack openly defies the interest and authority of the United Nations. Such an attack, therefore, concerns the vital interest which all the Member nations have in the Organization." [8]

Uniting for Peace

The ultimate significance of the first collective military action against aggression must be left to history. Its effect upon the evolution of the United Nations became apparent almost at once.

The Uniting for Peace Resolution, adopted by the General Assembly on November 3, 1950, signaled a maturing of the United Nations rather than an upheaval of structure.[9] It makes explicit the residual responsibility of the General Assembly for the maintenance of peace, if the Security Council "fails to exercise its primary responsibility" (Section A). The Assembly Rules of Procedure are, accordingly, amended

[8] S.C.O.R. (473rd mtng.), S/PV. 473 (1950).
[9] G.A. Resolution 377 (V), Sect. A.

by the resolution so as to facilitate the discharge of the Assembly's responsibility.

The Uniting for Peace Resolution establishes the Peace Observation Commission and the Collective Measures Committee, both of which are discussed more fully below. And it concludes with a reaffirmation of the Purposes and Principles of the Charter, coupled with a solemn exhortation to member states to intensify joint action in furtherance of the Charter aims.

The functions assigned by the Charter to the General Assembly relate to matters basic to the stability of international order. Moreover, the structure and processes of the Assembly can, if effectively used, further our own national interest in asserting power and principle through what Lester Pearson has called the "politics of arrangement." [10]

To the Assembly's direct responsibilities for peace and security, to which reference has been made, should be added its duty to recommend methods of promoting political cooperation and of developing international law (Article 13, para. 1[a]). It is also charged with promoting international cooperation in economic, social, cultural, educational, and health fields; assisting in the realization of human rights and fundamental freedoms; and bringing self-government or independence to inhabitants of territories under its trust and encouraging the progress of non-self-governing territories (Articles 13, para. 1[a], and Chapters IX, X, XI, XII). These tasks involve building ramparts against enemies of peace which are at least as ancient as force or duress, and are more fully discussed in Part II of this book.

Moreover, in view of the Security Council's abdication of its duty to formulate plans for the regulation of armaments (Article 26), increased importance attaches to the General Assembly's right to recommend "principles governing dis-

[10] "At this time, when the forces of social and political action can be as explosive as an uncontrolled nuclear reaction, we have nothing more certain to guide our progress than the politics of arrangement between nations and blocs of nations . . . there is no other practical focus for our aspirations." (Lester Pearson, Address at University of British Columbia, February 2, 1961, in *A Critical Evaluation of the United Nations* [Vancouver: University of British Columbia, 1961], p. 23.)

armament and the regulation of armaments" (Article 11, para. 1). For all practical purposes, the Assembly pre-empted the field in 1952 when it established a Disarmament Commission and the Security Council promptly accepted the Assembly's recommendation that it dissolve the Commission for Conventional Armaments and the Atomic Energy Commission.[11]

The General Assembly's authority in relation to peace and security has thus taken on major, rather than merely "residual," dimensions. This requires that its membership and its processes realistically reflect its tasks.

Universality

One of the major factors limiting the capacity of the United States to exert leadership in the United Nations arises from what may be called "the dilemma of the absent nations."

The Federal Republic of Germany has not sought admission to the United Nations, despite a growing feeling that the question of Germany will, in some form, be placed before the Organization. Although it is fully eligible for membership, the admission of the Federal Republic, like that of Korea and Viet-Nam, raises difficulties concerning the position of the Communist-controlled segments of these divided nations, inasmuch as the Soviet government has expressed its intention to veto the admission of the free portion of these states unless the Communist-dominated areas are admitted as well.

The issue of Chinese Communist participation in the United Nations becomes increasingly vexatious as our attitude of opposition to seating Red China in the United Nations diverges more and more from our probable capacity to influence the ultimate decision. Some members of the Organization, including, of course, the United States, regard the matter as involving a choice between moral principle and surrender to blackmail. Others, including some of our staunch allies, consider that to accord Red China representation in the

[11] G.A. Resolution 502 (VI), January 11, 1952; S.C. Resolution S/2506 (571st mtng.), January 30, 1952.

United Nations would be merely to accept a fact of international life.

To a large extent, these contending viewpoints reflect differing assumptions concerning the basic nature of the Organization itself. Should it be "universal," thus including all states? Should each member state be represented by the government in effective control of its people and territory? Or should representation be limited to states or governments ready and willing to carry out the Charter obligations? Are there, or should there be, states or governments to be regarded as outlaws in the international community?

All these questions received much attention at the San Francisco Conference. Agreement was ultimately reached that the participation of the original members was "acquired by right," whereas continued or new membership would be "dependent on the fulfillment of certain conditions." [12] There were, however, divergent points of view concerning both the right of charter members to remain in the Organization and the right of new applicants to join.

One group of delegations, led by Uruguay, stressed the importance of universality. They contended "that all communities should be members of the Organization and that their participation is obligatory." Hence any community—so long as it qualifies as a "state"—has no choice whether to become a member of the Organization or to withdraw from it. There would be no conditions for eligibility, nor any question of expulsion. The more evil the member, the more important that it be held to the obligations of the Charter and that it be kept in clear view of the nations. The majority of the delegations, however, rejected this point of view as impracticable at "the moment," though most conceded that universality "was an ideal toward which it was proper to aim."

At the same time, a long step was taken toward the principle of universality by cautioning all states to observe the Charter,

[12] See G.A., Special Committee on Admission of New Members, *Memorandum on . . . the Admission of New Members*, A/AC.64/1 (1953), pp. 6-18, which reflects the discussions on this subject and from which the ensuing quotations are derived.

irrespective of nonmembership. Article 2(6) imposes upon the Organization (that is to say, upon all members) a duty to "ensure that States which are not Members of the United Nations act in accordance with these Principles so far as may be necessary for the maintenance of international peace and security."

This principle is obviously relevant to even the most rudimentary world order. It was realized that otherwise the most ruthless offender could procure a license to carry on with impunity, merely by refusing to join the Organization or by withdrawing from membership, a right not precluded by the terms of the Charter.

For this reason, there was considerable opposition at San Francisco to the Dumbarton Oaks provision for expulsion of recalcitrant members. However, numerous delegations—and particularly the Soviet Union—insisted that it would be "unfortunate" to permit a persistent violator to remain a member.[13] The conference accordingly approved Article 6, providing for expulsion of members which persistently violated the Charter. The effect was largely negated, however, by subjecting such action to the veto.

The conference also adopted Article 4, requiring that new applicants be "peace-loving States which accept the obligations contained in the present Charter and, in the judgment of the Organization, are able and willing to carry out these obligations."

This principle was eroded by acceptance of the "package deal" in 1955, when sixteen states were admitted pursuant to one general resolution.[14] In view of the character of certain of these states, such as Albania, Hungary, Rumania, and Bulgaria, the Organization ignored Article 4 and expressed no judgment as to their ability or willingness to carry out their obligations.[15] The Assembly resolution limited itself to noting

[13] Secretary of State Edward R. Stettinius, Jr., "Report to the President on the Results of the San Francisco Conference" (June 26, 1945), in *The Charter of the United Nations,* cited, p. 61.

[14] G.A. Resolution 995 (X), December 4, 1955.

[15] In 1953, the U.S. Delegation, through James F. Byrnes, had opposed the package deal, saying: ". . . We cannot engage in bargaining where

a "general feeling in favor of the universality of the United Nations. . . ."

There is little doubt that this feeling is becoming ever more general, although with erratic incidence. Thus, the government of India has pressed for the seating of the People's Republic of China, but has not supported the admission of the Republic of Korea, a prime victim of Chinese aggression.

Attitudes of the member states regarding the Chinese representation question vary considerably and defy classification. As shown by the votes in the United Nations, most of the Asian and African governments favor seating Red China, or are not sufficiently interested to vote either way.

In the United States, on the other hand, it has only recently become possible even to raise the matter for public discussion without incurring charges of unworthy motive. Throughout American history the maintenance of a free and friendly China has been a fixed purpose of our foreign policy. Frustration of the policy by the Chinese Communists' seizure of the mainland was compounded by their wanton aggression in Korea. Deep emotion makes difficult an objective appraisal of Communist China's presence in the United Nations in terms of advantage and disadvantage to our national interest. The very discussion of the matter seems to many to imply a willingness to appease a declared enemy. Moreover, the anti-American campaigns of slander and threat conducted by Red China would undoubtedly make reversal of the United States' policy of nonrecognition of that regime and of opposition to its seating in the United Nations appear an abject surrender to blackmail.

For these reasons, it is not probable that in the foreseeable

the question is one of principle. . . . If under any package deal we now agree to admit them (the Soviet-sponsored applicants) we are saying they have become 'peace-loving' States. We cannot say that." (U.S. Delegation Press Release no. 1766, October 5, 1953.) Three years before, the governments of Bulgaria, Hungary, and Rumania had been condemned by the General Assembly itself for their willful refusal to fulfill their obligations under the peace treaties of 1947 and their callous indifference to the sentiments of the world community (G.A. Resolution 385 [V], November 3, 1950).

future the United States will—nor desirable that it should—modify its policy of opposing the seating of Communist China in any United Nations organ.

Above all, it is not to be forgotten that the preservation of the rights and freedoms of ten million people on the island of Taiwan is at stake. So long as the Communist government of China insists upon "liberation" of Taiwan as a precondition for taking a United Nations seat, that government is ordaining its own disqualification. Members of the Organization who speak loudly for the right of self-determination have here a prime opportunity to put principle into practice.

The United States in recent years has placed too much emphasis on the military posture of Taiwan and too little upon the necessity for strengthening the economy and broadening the base of government on the island. There is no reason why Taiwan could not become a showcase of democracy for all of Asia, as well as continue to serve the free world as an "unsinkable aircraft carrier."

Debate and Negotiation

The major peace-keeping responsibilities of the Assembly require not only a realistic appraisal of the "membership" question, but, in addition, renewed efforts to improve its method of work and to strengthen its peace-keeping machinery.

Reference has been made to the 1947 proposal for the establishment of an Interim Committee of the General Assembly. The functions envisaged for the Committee were: (1) to help the Assembly prepare for its next regular session; (2) to follow up actions recommended by the previous Assembly; (3) to assist in formulation of principles on matters within the authority of the Assembly, such as disarmament and the development of international law; (4) to conduct investigations or appoint commissions of inquiry within the scope of its duties.

Although the Interim Committee has been abortive because of Soviet boycott, the needs which gave rise to it in the first place have increased. Nevertheless, the members have not given a high priority to the search for practical alternatives.

Efforts to improve the Assembly's method of work through limitation or regulation of debate have foundered on the rock of "sovereign equality." Such efforts have been rejected by those who prefer less ordered democratic processes to disciplined and inevitably more authoritarian ones.[16]

United Nations discussions on the subject of limiting public debate illuminate the political significance of debate as compared with private negotiation. Freedom of debate in an open forum serves the weaker party; private discussion normally favors the side with the greater capacity to impose its will, since it facilitates recourse to threat or covert pressures.

The diplomatic uses of debate and negotiation may be mutually exclusive, complementary, or even identical, depending upon the intention of one or another of the participants. If the primary purpose is to influence the opinion or action of third parties, the process is more accurately described as "debate" than "negotiation."

For this reason, summit meetings normally have the character of debate. Soviet leaders have been more concerned with influencing opinion across the world than across the table. They have profited from a widespread sense of frustration when spotlighted "negotiations" break down and deadlock is dramatized. It might help to restore public perspective on this matter to remember that, although negotiations "fail" if they end in deadlock, debates take place for the very purpose of exposing the reasons for deadlock. If it had been the purpose of Lincoln and Douglas to influence each other, rather than their listeners, history would have recorded their encounter as an abortive negotiation, rather than a highly successful debate.

Furthermore, in all advanced systems of law, agreements reached as the result of duress are voidable and unenforceable. Even in the rudimentary state of international order, where

---

[16] Thus, attempts to enlarge the powers of presiding officers, made at the Fourth, Seventh, and Eighth Sessions, led to eloquent pleas for the "inalienable right" of members freely to express their views. (*Repertory of United Nations Practice* [New York: United Nations, 1955], v. 1, p. 627.) Although the membership has since doubled, heightening the need for devices to limit debate, efforts along this line are still resisted.

treaties are valid even if coerced, it makes no sense to describe discussions held at gun point as a form of "negotiation." Concessions demanded through undue pressure or the use of force are most fairly dealt with by exposing the issues to debate, so that counterpressures may be generated which, perhaps, can aid in creating conditions making genuine negotiation possible. A recent example is Soviet retreat from insistence upon the "troika" in the face of the overwhelming opposition reflected in the United Nations debates on the issue.

Unfortunately, many smaller powers tend to regard "talks" between antagonists as ends in themselves. Nonaligned nations often press for "negotiation" between the great powers, while remaining noncommittal concerning the merits of issues in dispute between them. Thus, the brutal suddenness of Soviet resumption of nuclear tests in September 1961, on the eve of the Belgrade Conference, precipitated anxious demands for "negotiation." [17] Yet history shows that "negotiation" is not in itself an alternative to war or other forms of violence. Discussions were taking place when bombs fell on Pearl Harbor. Munich was a preliminary to aggression. When uncommitted states press for negotiation between the great powers, with little regard to the merit or moral content of issues, the pressures fall most heavily upon the more tractable side. Indeed, such pressures often become the unwitting partner of extortion.

The very fact that debate normally involves "taking sides" is a prime characteristic of the parliamentary process, and its highest justification for existence. The small nations could lose most if they were to use the Assembly merely as a convenient forum in which to express their own parochial and limited interests. Such a course would deprive the Organization of much of its value as a means for giving effect to the common interest of all nations, large and small, in loyal compliance with the Charter.

The *Congressional Record* contains numerous reports of

---

[17] For example, Prime Minister Nehru, although declining to offer suggestions as to means of settling the Berlin dispute, warned: "There is no choice left between negotiations or war." (*The New York Times*, September 3, 1961.)

lengthy debates in which the United Nations is derided as a "debating society." Tolerance with the workings of familiar home institutions does not preclude criticism of similar characteristics of alien ones. Nevertheless, the function of debate is identical in all parliamentary bodies, international or national: the formation of public understanding, without which no society can discipline itself.

Disarmament

These considerations are particularly true with regard to the perennial problem of the regulation and control of armaments. World opinion is acutely conscious, particularly in the aftermath of megaton nuclear testing, of the peril of mutual suicide if nations should leap—or stumble—into war. However, there is little understanding of the problems involved in controlling new weapons or delivery systems, or in the elusive quest for stability through mutual deterrence.

Analysis of the complex problem of disarmament is beyond the scope and competence of the present work. Nevertheless, certain aspects of our present position are relevant to an appraisal of the use of the United Nations as a forum for informing the public judgment concerning issues of war, peace, and survival.

The Soviet government has sought to exploit popular fear and confusion by holding out the lure of "general and complete disarmament." Like other well-worn phrases of the cold war armory such as "peaceful coexistence," this device conveys a hazy impression of a goal which, though ultimate, is yet somehow capable of immediate achievement. The slogan is, in fact, the epitome of the Soviet "all-or-nothing" approach to disarmament.

Even as recently as 1955 the Soviet government did not think it expedient to disinter the plan which Litvinov had put forward in the League of Nations over thirty years before, labeled "Immediate, Complete and General Disarmament," a proposal that was ridiculed and abandoned. Soviet Foreign Minister Molotov introduced new Soviet disarmament proposals of 1955 with the forthright admission: "The problem of disarmament or *to put it more precisely, the problem of the reduction of armaments . . .*" He thus deferred to an informed public opinion, which years of U.S. effort in the United Nations had succeeded in marshaling in support of a realistic and guarded—though unsensational—approach. U.S. objectives were well summarized in 1952: "An effective system of progressive and continuing disclosure and verification of all armed forces and armaments, including atomic, to achieve the open world in which alone there can be effective disarmament." [18]

The indispensable element of the "open world" is lost from sight in the hazy allure of "general and complete disarmament." The word "immediate" was eliminated by Mr. Khrushchev from the Litvinov formula when he presented his comprehensive "new" plan to the United Nations in 1959, no doubt as a concession to plausibility. But his proposal of a "four-year" target—also taken, incidentally, from the Litvinov proposals of 1927-28—was more a gesture of propaganda than of practical reality. Far from elucidating the true nature of the problem, the unrealistic timetable, like the phrase "general and complete," is designed to divert public attention from some hard facts of life.

One is that economic and industrial power comprises the foundation of war-making potential. This involves a capacity for speedy conversion of tractors into tanks, airliners into bombers, and fissionable material into weapons, and is the backbone of "armaments." Furthermore, the Soviet proposal that "governments discontinue . . . appropriation of funds for military purposes in any form," is part of the fraud; even if given specific content, it could be policed only in an open and self-disciplining society.

Moreover, the rarely mentioned but vastly destructive potential of chemical-biological-radiological warfare presents almost insuperable problems of control and inspection over production, stockpiling or delivery systems; hence their elimi-

[18] U.S. Proposal in Disarmament Commission (April 24, 1952), U.N. Disarmament Commission, *Official Records: Special Supplement 1, Second Report of the Disarmament Commission*, DC/20 (New York, 1952), pp. 84-85.

nation is highly problematical.[19] And the Soviets themselves have conceded the impossibility of detecting already secreted stockpiles of nuclear arms.

It is, therefore, a matter for some concern that the United States has adopted what President Kennedy, in his speech to the United Nations in September 1961, described as "the label both nations now accept." [20]

It is essential to make full use of all United Nations facilities—as well as other available media of information—to restore public perspectives on this matter. President Kennedy made wise use of the forum of the General Assembly when he pointed out, in the same speech, that destruction of arms is not an end in itself and that we must create "world-wide law and law enforcement as we outlaw world-wide war and weapons. . . . For peace is not solely a matter of military or technical problems, it is primarily a problem of politics and people." [21]

The relationship between scaling down armaments and building up peace-keeping machinery was emphasized also in a U.S. memorandum submitted to the Assembly. Any program of disarmament, it stated, "which does not embody this relationship is a program for disorder and the perpetuation of disputes among nations. Nations which are expected to give up their means of self-protection must have available other effective means of safeguarding their legitimate interests." [22] It cannot be overstressed that the quest for disarmament is essentially another way of describing the age-old search for alternatives to war.

Another illustration of effective use of the General Assembly for education and stimulation to action was the initiative of

[19] See, for example, *Chemical-Biological-Radiological (CBR) Warfare and its Disarmament Aspects,* a study prepared by the Subcommittee on Disarmament of the Senate Committee on Foreign Relations, Committee print, 86th Cong., 2d sess. (Washington: GPO, 1960).

[20] September 25; full text in *The New York Times,* September 26, 1961.

[21] Same.

[22] U.S. Disarmament Administration, *Memorandum on Principles That Should Govern Negotiations for General and Complete Disarmament in a Peaceful World,* Disarmament Document Series, no. 27, September 19, 1961, p. 3.

former President Eisenhower in his "Atoms for Peace" speech on December 8, 1953. His proposal for the establishment of an International Atomic Energy Agency bore fruit when, three years later, a statute for such an agency emerged from arduous sessions, which were in themselves models of intensive and intelligent negotiation, for which high credit is due to the U.S. Delegation under the leadership of Ambassador James J. Wadsworth.

The General Assembly is by far the best available forum for clarifying the basic issues underlying the problem of disarmament and exposing oversimplifications and illusions. The same is true of other great problems of war and peace as well.

Leaders of some of the great powers have lamented on occasion that they could wield greater influence and persuasion if only they were unhampered by nations of little power or men of lesser stature. But the great powers have no mandate to assume the directing role. Efforts to "manage" popular assemblages place too high a premium on the wisdom of the managers.[23] At the same time, availability of a forum for free debate places an equally high premium on the capacity for self-discipline.

The United States should, both by precept and practice, point out the harm which may be done by unrestrained or strident uses of the forum. On many occasions, ill-timed and ill-mannered debate has inflamed tension and provoked disagreement. The Charter itself foresaw such dangers, exhorting parties to disputes, *"first of all,"* to seek a solution by peaceful means of their own choice (Article 33). New emphasis on this Charter provision would be salutary for the strengthening of the United Nations as a mediatory agency, rather than a mere cyclone cellar.

Texts of resolutions, and the voting on them, have the appeal of headlines and box scores. It seems easy to see who

[23] Thus, even so respected a leader as President de Gaulle has encountered resistance to his efforts to "organize an objective debate" in the French National Assembly, as he proposed should be done in the United Nations, despite the powerful means which the constitution of the Fifth Republic gives the President to block or control parliamentary action.

"won" and who "lost" without the need to bother about the issues in dispute. Nevertheless, the compulsive effects of General Assembly resolutions are directly related to the clarity with which they are formulated and to the will with which they are followed up by the membership. And it is often observed that adjournment of debate may be more constructive than pressing matters to a "conclusion."

Nothing could be more self-evident than the proposition that, in a body composed of more than one hundred members, rather than half that number, difficulty increases—perhaps in geometric proportion—in maintaining order, marshaling sentiment, and inducing effective action. Furthermore, the traditional tendency of large powers to regard responsibility as a direct function of size clashes with the equal and opposite tendency of smaller nations to assume that differences between the large nations inevitably reflect conflicts of power rather than of principle.

Nonaligned Members

Smaller nations are likely to bring this perspective into sharp focus through the parliamentary processes of debate and vote. "Neutralism," in United Nations terms, often takes the form of selective abstention. The right to abstain becomes a manifestation of the power to show either indifference or disapproval. At the same time, although nonalignment may be motivated by considerations of narrow self-interest or weakness, leaders of many nonaligned nations often genuinely seek to apply Woodrow Wilson's dictum: "The basis of neutrality is not indifference, it is not self-interest. . . . It is impartiality of spirit and of judgment."

Involved as we are in a duel with the Communist powers on matters of fundamental principle, it is natural to regard neutral attitudes as akin to betrayal of American interests and of the Charter's purposes and principles. It may salve the pride to react with demands that "the boys be separated from the men." The dilemma is that the louder we protest, the more significance we lend to the voting process, and refusal to make a public commitment seems all the more alluring to smaller nations as a means of demonstrating their "independence."

Weighted Voting

Among the parliamentary devices proposed for dealing with problems posed by nonparticipation in decisions, by relatively small contribution to the common effort, or by the continuing influx of small and inexperienced nations as new members, is that of the weighted vote. Analogy is drawn to voting procedures built into technical or single-purpose agencies, such as the International Bank for Reconstruction and Development, and organizations established for reaching decisions concerning tariff rates, international commodity quotas and prices, and the like.

Considerations applicable to weighted voting in technical organs differ in several respects from those in political organs, such as the General Assembly. One difference is that, in the former, general consent to action through weighted majority rule often reflects the simple fact that in such agencies the larger contributors or participants would not contribute or participate on any other basis. This is manifestly not the case with respect to parliamentary political organs. The distinction is basically the same as that between the one-man-one-vote rule in a political body such as the Congress of the United States, as compared with the accepted practice of giving to a shareholder the right to cast one vote for each share of stock he owns in a stock corporation.

Moreover, fair standards for weighting the vote are readily ascertainable in the case of most technical agencies. An organization to fix sugar quotas logically weights voting rights on the basis of comparative statistics of sugar production or consumption. On the other hand, methods proposed for weighting the vote in United Nations political bodies often have the intricacy of an electronic computer.[24]

[24] The United World Federalists, for example, once proposed that the Assembly voting system should be based on population, literacy, and industrial development, and be reassessed at three- or five-year intervals.

Furthermore, vote-weighting in bodies with broad political functions would not serve—and might, indeed, even disserve—its intended purpose. As Secretary-General Hammarskjold once remarked, General Assembly resolutions frequently "reflect only part of what has, in fact, emerged from deliberations and what, therefore, is likely to remain as an active element in future developments." The moral and political dimensions of a resolution are to be measured by its content, its clarity of meaning, its sponsorship and the identity and purpose of those who do not merely vote for it, but follow through to its execution.

Improvement of Peace-Keeping Processes

There are, however, other organizational devices which could generate self-discipline in the uses of the forum. Thus, a standing committee, composed of former Presidents of the General Assembly and assisted by Secretariat staff, might be established to survey Assembly procedures. Annual Reports submitted to the Assembly by such a group would serve as the basis for continuing self-study, upon which self-discipline rests.

The adequate staffing of permanent missions is, of course, also an essential aspect of this matter, since overburdened delegations cannot possibly obtain information or maintain contact essential to effective use of the forum.

Furthermore, the United States (along with the membership as a whole) tends to regard the General Assembly as a three-month spectacle, which folds its tents at season's end and goes into winter quarters. The quantity, range, and complexity of the agenda of the General Assembly require that the diplomatic show be kept on the road all year round. To

(Testimony of Cord Meyer, Jr. [May 11, 1948], *Structure of the United Nations and the Relations of the United States to the United Nations*, Hearings before the House Committee on Foreign Affairs, 80th Cong., 2d sess., May 4-14, 1948 [Washington: GPO, 1948], pp. 208, 213.) For the Security Council Ely Culbertson's "ABC Plan" urged abolition of the veto, in favor of giving two votes each to the U.S.S.R., United Kingdom and United States, one each to France and China, and two votes collectively to the smaller members; any six votes being sufficient for a decision.

this end, between sessions of the Assembly, all United States diplomatic missions should be given a continuing responsibility to help prepare for the next session and to follow through on the recommendations of the prior one. They could, in this practical manner, pick up at least part of the function envisaged for the defunct Interim Committee. The more important U.S. Embassies might be provided with an Officer for United Nations Affairs, who would supervise all multilateral activities and programs falling within the scope of the Embassy's duties. Such a procedure could assure continuous contact on these matters between the Department of State and U.S. diplomatic missions.

Finally, the United States should take the lead in efforts to strengthen the standing mechanisms through which the General Assembly can discharge its peace-keeping functions.

Peace Observation and Enforcement

These functions include observation and reporting on situations threatening peace, as well as procedures for collective measures if the peace is broken. The Peace Observation Commission was accepted by all members, including the U.S.S.R., as an important instrument for keeping the membership informed concerning situations which might imperil peace. The Soviet Union objected, on constitutional grounds, to devices such as the Interim Committee, designed to strengthen the United Nations' muscle. In their wisdom, the Kremlin leaders nevertheless saw no legal difficulty in improving the United Nations' senses of sight and hearing. It is therefore all the more surprising that the Commission has been employed only once,[25] and that it has been dormant ever since. One explanation for the shelving of the P.O.C. is that it has not been composed at a sufficiently high level. Another is that its intended functions have been largely taken over by the Secretary-Gen-

[25] In 1951, it established a Balkan subcommission pursuant to G.A. Resolution 508 (VI), December 7, 1951, and sent a team to Yugoslavia's frontiers, threatened by aggression from the Soviet bloc.

eral, in view of the close connection between observation and conciliation.

Nevertheless, much value might be derived from a modernized, upgraded P.O.C. One difficulty in the way of its use might be removed by authorizing such a Commission to initiate investigations, which now require resolutions adopted by two-thirds of the Assembly membership, or decisions by the veto-bound Security Council.[26] Furthermore, in the light of experience showing the interconnection between fact-finding and peace-making, study should be given to the practicability of adding a good-offices function to the Commission's authority. Such renovation of the P.O.C. might lead to its activation as a standing group from which the Secretary-General could compose missions for use in situations which hitherto have called for a "United Nations presence." In view of the benefits which flowed from the precedents set by the late Secretary-General in delegating representatives to serve in Laos, Jordan, and elsewhere, there would seem to be potential value in making the services of the P.O.C. available to him upon his own initiative without prior consent of the General Assembly or Security Council.

Furthermore, if the Peace Observation Commission is revitalized, it could be designated by the General Assembly to serve as the parent body for a Peace Observation Force, designed to carry out police and guard functions in areas of tension or international concern. Observation and policing are closely interrelated functions.

Experience in the Middle East and the Congo has, of course, confirmed how real is the lurking threat of great-power military involvement in troubled areas. Soviet efforts to make the Congo a "happy hunting ground of the cold war," in Mr. Hammarskjold's phrase, lend a dual significance to the presence of units supplied by the smaller nations: they not only observe and patrol the area itself; their very presence deprives the big powers of a pretext for intrusion.

A Peace Observation Force could, accordingly, be made up of armed and mobile contingents whose character and com-

[26] The Commission could not in any event go into an area without the invitation or consent of the state concerned.

position in a particular case would depend upon the intended use. There would be no "standing force," although a permanent United Nations Command or Staff of small dimensions could serve usefully for contingency planning, for advising how suitable units might be trained and earmarked, and, in the event of need, for procuring requisite logistical support.

The disarmament proposals introduced by the United States at the outset of the Sixteenth General Assembly contemplate the establishment of a United Nations Peace Force composed of national contingents, including units furnished by the great powers.[27] In fact, prior to the introduction of these proposals in September 1961, no serious suggestion had been made since 1947 for resuming negotiations regarding agreement to make armed forces available to the Security Council in accordance with Chapter VII (Article 43) of the Charter.

In May 1960, on the eve of the abortive summit meeting, Mr. Hammarskjold took occasion to comment upon then current suggestions for supplementing disarmament arrangements by an international force. He pointed out that ". . . If and when the parties to disarmament were to reach the conclusion that there is a need for some kind of international policing, it should in my view first of all call for the reconsideration of Chapter VII. . . . If there is considered to be a snag in Chapter VII which makes it impossible to reach implementation, one should of course study whatever revisions of Chapter VII might meet the new situation." [28]

This was intended as a warning against the tendency of member nations to deal with difficult problems, including disarmament, as if answers could by some magic be found outside the framework of the United Nations, or through formulas not envisaged by the Charter.

The original design for giving the United Nations a "preponderance of power for peace," in Ambassador Warren R. Austin's alliterative phrase, was one of the earliest casualties

---

[27] *The New York Times,* September 26, 1961, sets forth the text in full; G.A. (16th sess.), *Letter Dated 25 September 1961 from the Representative of the United States . . . to the President of the General Assembly,* A/4891 (1961).

[28] Press Conference of May 5, 1960; Note no. 1266.

of the cold war, that is to say, of the Soviet revolt against the Charter. Accordingly, an agreement to bring Article 43 to life would signal an astonishing reversal of Soviet foreign policy. Moreover, such an ostensible arrangement might well prove illusory inasmuch as the actual availability of armed forces in particular situations would remain subject to the veto. Any aggressor state could in fact act with impunity, if only it were acting for, or on sufferance of, a permanent member of the Security Council.

It is essential to avoid confusing cause with effect on this matter. The reason why Chapter VII has lain dormant is precisely the same reason why the foundations of the United Nations itself are being undermined through abuse of the veto. The answer is to be found not in lack of ingenious formulas, but in the many tactics and devices by which the Soviet government has obstructed the purposes of the Charter.

It is not the absence of "peace forces" which strains relations between nations. Tensions are caused by disparate moral values, divergent notions of cooperation and coexistence, and clash of political aims at specific points on the globe.

However regrettable the fact may be, prospects of an international police force are remote. If the creation of such a force is made a precondition of progress in the field of disarmament, then the latter also becomes a remote prospect. If confirmation of this estimate is needed, it may be found in the difficulties encountered in financing the United Nations Congo force, despite the urgent and obvious necessities.

The current U.S. disarmament program also, and more realistically, envisages the creation of a United Nations "peace observation group," with a "standing cadre of observers." Advance planning for a Peace Observation Force, and the establishment of a central United Nations Staff and Command Post would be practicable and wholly consistent with the long-neglected recommendations of the Collective Measures Committee.

One of the most comprehensive studies ever made of the anatomy of collective security is to be found in the First Report of that Committee, released in 1951.[29] A copy might well be placed on the desk of every delegation at the opening of each General Assembly.

One conclusion of the Report—it is, in fact, a warning—is that "whatever economic, financial and military measures may be taken will depend for their effectiveness upon the speed and completeness with which they are applied." [30] The Report recommends that states take such preparatory steps as: maintenance of elements within their armed forces, trained, organized and equipped so as to be available for service as United Nations units; adoption of legislative and administrative regulations to facilitate prompt collective action, when needed; formulation of plans for joint economic measures which would assure effective action and a fair sharing of burdens.

The apathy of governments, regrettably including the United States, toward these recommendations shows how far we are from the most rudimentary system of collective security, which presupposes the capacity to concert will power even more than fire power. It is to be hoped that the United States will now resume leadership in efforts to persuade nations to accept the long-dormant recommendations of the Collective Measures Committee. Indeed, in President Kennedy's address before the General Assembly on September 25, 1961,[31] he sounded the first call heard in many years for such action. Although he did not refer to the Committee's Report by name, he urged, ". . . that all member nations earmark special peace-keeping units in their armed forces, to be on call to the United Nations, to be specially trained and quickly available —and with advance provision for financial and logistic support."

It is to be hoped that this reaffirmation of the recommendations of the Committee may lead to action. The United States

[29] The Committee was established under the Uniting for Peace Resolution, G.A. Resolution 377 (V), Sect. C, November 3, 1950. Its First Report was circulated as G.A.O.R. (6th sess.), *Supplement 13, Report of the Collective Measures Committee,* A/1891 (1951).

[30] Report, cited, para. 33.

[31] *The New York Times,* September 26, 1961.

itself might well, though belatedly, comply with the recommendations, as an inducement for others to follow suit.

Forty years ago the League of Nations adopted explicit "Resolutions on the Economic Weapon." [32] These were designed to give effect to Article XVI of the Covenant, imposing the obligation upon members immediately to sever all economic and financial intercourse with a state resorting to war in violation of the Covenant. They were reasonably good resolutions, on the books a full fourteen years before the Italian aggression against Ethiopia. When the testing-time came, however, it was proved once again that a resolution is not enough; what is essential is resolve.

The lesson should be required reading for proponents of world government, or others whose blueprints for a new ark divert attention from the need to repair the raft on which we must ride the flood.

[32] League of Nations, *The Records of the Second Assembly: Plenary Meetings . . . 5th of September to the 5th of October, 1921* (Geneva, 1921), 21st meeting, p. 450 ff., and 30th meeting, p. 808 ff.

Part II

BUILDING A JUST ORDER

Chapter IV

Economic Foundations of Peace

The end of World War II brought to a close three great enterprises of international cooperation.

The first was the wartime coalition itself; the second, the mightiest military establishment in history; and the third, the program of mutual aid known as "Lend-Lease," under which fifty billion dollars worth of "defense articles," including food, was provided by the United States to forty-five allies. These, in turn, reciprocated by contributing eight billion dollars worth of their own.

The coalition dissolved into an implacable conflict of wills and ideas, the outcome of which is not foreseeable. The military establishment was hastily dismantled, at any rate by the Western segment of the coalition, only to be rebuilt within a few years in response to aggression in Korea. And Lend-Lease was abruptly terminated, to be replaced in revised form and for different objectives, first by the United Nations Relief and Rehabilitation Administration (UNRRA), and then by the United Nations itself, including the Specialized Agencies. Certain of these, notably the Food and Agriculture Organization and the International Bank, had come into being even before the war's end.

In planned sequence, economic cooperation was directed first at successful prosecution of the war, then at healing the ravages of war and, finally, at building the economic foundations of peace.

As early as September 1941 the governments-in-exile in London had formed a committee to prepare for the needs of postwar relief and reconstruction. The United States attended its sessions, even prior to Pearl Harbor; thereafter we participated actively. Largely as a result of this foresight, UNRRA was able to ship twenty million tons of supplies to some fifteen nations during the first two years following the war. In 1946, the UNRRA Council met to terminate the Organization and to transfer many of its tasks to permanent international agencies: health activities to the World Health Organization; care of displaced persons to the International Refugee Organization; care of children in the liberated areas of Europe and Asia to the newly created International Children's Fund. Other activities were left for the United Nations Assembly to deal with as it saw fit.

UNRRA's purpose of averting famine and chaos in the liberated areas led to an unprecedented cooperative peacetime effort. The United States itself, which had been the major contributor to UNRRA, has since continued through its own foreign aid program to bear the largest burden of economic and financial assistance to countries unable to put their own economies into motion.

At the same time, the United States led in the creation of the permanent machinery of the United Nations, set up to foster development of the world's natural and human resources and to create conditions indispensable to individual dignity and human freedom. This machinery and these purposes, likewise, had been envisaged since the early days of the war.

There is no historic parallel to the intensive effort with which nations, in the dark hours of war, prepared for political, economic and social problems to be faced at an uncertain time in an unknown future. It was an act of faith and of responsibility.

The fact that such efforts took place not as an "answer to communism," but during the high period of coalition, illuminates a simple truth: it would be just as necessary to build economic and social foundations of order and progress even if, by a double miracle, the Soviet system were to turn overnight into a model parliamentary democracy and the Chinese Communists were suddenly to conform to normal standards of behavior.

The heavy burden assumed by the people of the United States in support of foreign economic and technical assistance programs obviously calls for a careful choice of procedures by which our objectives and expenditures can best be rewarded.

Over-ardent supporters of the United Nations tend to claim for the Organization a right of way. Others have stressed the merits of the regional or the bilateral method. Some successful programs, such as the Colombo Plan, are based upon coordinated bilateral agreements. On the other hand, regional arrangements for economic development have lost some of their first bloom, as, for example, the failure of Article 2 of the North Atlantic Treaty to serve as a vehicle for "economic collaboration" among the parties. The Alliance for Progress, true to the tradition of hemispheric understanding, may well prove to be an illustrious exception.

The inference to be drawn from the experience of postwar years is that no institutional arrangement as such is entitled to claim a priority. A more functional approach is necessary, involving realistic appraisal of the nature of economic problems and the ways in which international programs and processes can best respond to them. Major questions now arise with respect to the less developed and emergent states.

Consideration of the disparate range of problems confronting these states shows at once that no single institution, procedure or arrangement could possibly do the job alone. Rates of economic growth almost uniformly diminish in these societies in relation to population increases. Local enterprise, management, and skills are lacking. Political and social dislocations, often involving class conflict if not revolution, make orderly investment and trade difficult. In many cases, a single crop or mineral accounts for the major economic return. The late Secretary-General frequently pointed out that the fluctuations in prices of these primary products involved income and foreign exchange losses in excess of all foreign assistance programs combined.

So far as the United States is concerned, it seems obvious that by far the major share of our contribution to programs designed to help solve such problems as these will continue to be on a bilateral basis, or at least one in which the U.S. government will arrange basic terms, even if multilateral agencies or foreign governments also participate. An example is the financing of the Volta River Dam project in Ghana, involving long-term loans by the United States, the International Bank and the British government, in addition to credits by private enterprise.

Choice among available bilateral, regional or United Nations channels involves an application of pragmatic tests, rather than abstract principles. It is well established by experience that multilateral administration of certain types of programs returns a higher yield per dollar than bilateral programs. The United Nations, or its specialized agencies, are often in a better position to impose conditions and controls which, in the case of bilateral programs, might arouse charges of "strings" or "intervention."

So far as concerns the organization of multilateral processes and institutions, two broad concepts have emerged. One of these favors a centralized system which is closely related to, if not embodied in, the United Nations itself. The other prefers specialized operations through autonomous, though coordinated, agencies.

U.N. Organizations and Programs

The Charter of the United Nations gives a high place to international economic cooperation in the struggle to achieve a just order.[1] The sponsoring powers at San Francisco, speaking through John Foster Dulles, explained that the principle of "domestic jurisdiction" was ". . . now broadened to include functions which would enable the Organization to eradi-

---

[1] Article 55 calls for promoting: "(a) higher standards of living, full employment, and conditions of economic and social progress and development; (b) solutions of international economic, social health and related problems; and international cultural and educational cooperation. . . ."

cate the underlying causes of war as well as to deal with economic and social problems. . . ." [2]

In order to give effect to this mandate, the Charter provided for the Economic and Social Council, and for the necessary continuing work in this field there were created the Economic and Social Departments of the United Nations Secretariat and later four regional economic commissions—for Europe, Asia and the Far East, Latin America, and Africa. These commissions are served by staffs integrated in the U.N. Secretariat and financed directly through the United Nations budget.

Similarly under central direction—though organized as special operations—are the U.N. Children's Fund (1946), U.N. Relief and Works Agency for Palestine Refugees (1949), and the U.N. High Commissioner for Refugees (1950).

In January 1959, the United Nations Special Fund began operations, giving new emphasis to what its director, Paul G. Hoffman, described as "preinvestment" projects, such as surveys of resources and of the feasibility of basic development, training in crafts and skills, and research to find new commercial uses of available materials.

Some of its projects have arisen from the U.N. Expanded Program of Technical Assistance. The latter program has been one of the most dramatic activities of the United Nations which, in collaboration with a number of the Specialized Agencies, has expended $235 million voluntarily contributed since 1950 by eighty-five governments.[3]

Industrial programing has been recognized as of sufficient importance to warrant the creation of an Industrial Development Center within the United Nations Secretariat.

With regard to grants of aid, the recently established International Development Association is a beginning toward meeting requirements of capital for basic development projects not

[2] *Documents of the United Nations Conference on International Organization, San Francisco, 1945,* v. 6: *Commission I: General Provisions* (London and New York: U.N. Information Organizations, 1945), p. 507.

[3] See Paul G. Hoffman, *One Hundred Countries: One and One Quarter Billion People* (Washington: Committee for International Economic Growth, for the Lasker Foundation, 1960), pp. 36-43.

regarded as "bankable" by the International Bank. These will presumably include such activities as water supply, housing, railways and other projects which would not be immediately revenue-producing or otherwise directly productive in a financial sense.

The United Nations Secretariat—again in coordination with Specialized Agencies—also assists in programs for education and training in the developing countries, as well as for the application of science and technology. The Scientific Advisory Committee of the Secretariat has called for an international conference on this subject.

Finally, increasing value is being derived from a program to which the late Secretary-General attached much importance: that of providing operational, executive, and administrative personnel to less developed countries requesting such assistance. This service, known as OPEX, finds persons from various parts of the world qualified to serve the new states in public administration, economic development, postal services, social welfare and other public functions. In this area, as in most others, the Specialized Agencies also provide similar services within their own fields of competence.

A symptom of the importance attached to all these programs is the pressure of the new members for enlargement of the Economic and Social Council, giving greater voice to Asia and Africa. This body is designated by the Charter a "principal organ of the United Nations," and is responsible to plan and oversee all its peace-building activities: promotion of international cooperation for higher standards of living, observance of human rights, and all other matters pertaining to the general welfare of the nations (Article 62). It would seem logical that, if its membership was appropriately set at eighteen when the total United Nations membership was fifty, the Council should be expanded—although not necessarily proportionately—now that the total membership has more than doubled. Such a change, however, requires an amendment to the Charter, and the Soviet Union has repeatedly warned of its intention to veto any such amendments until the Chinese representation question is "solved."

Secretary-General Hammarskjold, in his 1959 report to the General Assembly,[4] urged upon members the importance of organizing the work of the Economic and Social Council so as to enable it to discuss "issues of decisive general importance at a policy-making level." He suggested this might be done at short special meetings of ministers. Mr. Hammarskjold might well have intended this to be a gentle warning lest the Council's work descend to routine technical levels, thus impeding the United Nations, in his words, from "playing a role of the same significance in the economic field as the one which is entrusted to it in the political sphere." The United States might well take an initiative in carrying out this recommendation.

Specialized Agencies

The concept of autonomous, though coordinated, operations has found expression in the development of the Specialized Agencies. Each has its own organic act, separate governing body, headquarters, secretariat, budget and program.

When the United Nations was established, some of these agencies already had a long history of operations. Indeed, the International Telecommunication Union (founded in 1865 under another name) will soon be celebrating its centennial. Two others—the Universal Postal Union (1875) and the World Meteorological Organization (1878)—have been at work for over eighty years. The International Labor Organization (1919) was a child of World War I. Several of the later organizations were based—in part—on the work of earlier prototypes.

Conferences held during World War II led to the establishment of the Food and Agriculture Organization (1945), the International Bank for Reconstruction and Development (1945), the International Monetary Fund (1945) and the International Civil Aviation Organization (1947). The United Na-

[4] G.A.O.R. (14th sess.), *Supplement 1A, Introduction to the Annual Report of the Secretary-General on the Work of the Organization, 16 June 1958-15 June 1959*, A/4132/Add. 1 (1959), p. 3.

tions Education, Scientific, and Cultural Organization came into being in 1946, and the World Health Organization the following year (both of these reflecting the pattern of their precursors in the period of the League of Nations). These were followed by the International Finance Corporation (1956), the International Atomic Energy Agency (1957), the Inter-Governmental Maritime Consultative Organization (1959), and the International Development Association (1960).

The multiplicity of agencies in the United Nations system, and the confusion implicit in working simultaneously on two divergent principles of organization, raise questions concerning the efficiency of such an arrangement. Administrative overhead is high, and there is unavoidable jurisdictional friction, as well as duplication of effort. There would be obvious advantages in greater integration and central budgetary and administrative controls. Resistance to what the agencies call "undue centralization" reflects a somewhat parochial attitude.

There are, nevertheless, valid reasons for preserving the individuality of the Specialized Agencies as technical organs, operating with relative freedom from political pressures which bear down upon the United Nations itself. The Agencies are able to marshal world-wide professional resources in their own special fields more successfully than could any all-embracing central organization. Moreover, they offer membership to states such as Switzerland and the Federal Republic of Germany which are not members of the United Nations. Autonomy often shelters their budgets from political controversy, such as that which attends the United Nations Congo operations.

The separate status of the Specialized Agencies does not, however, guarantee immunity from ideological conflict. An example is the dispute concerning trade-unionism in the I.L.O. and the refusal of certain employer associations in the United States to participate. Nevertheless, the Agencies do enjoy a measure of political insulation and, accordingly, are relatively more free to deal with technical questions on their merits.

The controversy over the appointment of a new Director-General of the International Atomic Energy Agency, to succeed Sterling Cole, demonstrates that politically rough weather is unavoidable in any organization of which the Soviet Union is a member. By contrast, the fact that the Soviets do not participate in the International Bank for Reconstruction and Development has facilitated the efficient, workmanlike functioning of that agency, with relative freedom from political distractions.

The absence of veto power over the appointment of the executive heads of the Specialized Agencies, moreover, spares them in any event from the kind of attack upon the integrity of executive leadership which the Soviets are now launching against the United Nations itself. If the executive and administrative functions of the Specialized Agencies are permitted to escape the corrosive effects of such assaults, they could serve as ramparts for the defense of the principle of an international civil service.

The case for independent existence of the Specialized Agencies has been well expressed by the Director-General of the Food and Agriculture Organization, who stated that the functional character of Specialized Agencies arises no doubt from the desire of the United Nations to provide the maximum chance of success in international cooperation in technical fields by removing it as far as possible from political influence and control. That is why each Specialized Agency has its own charter, its own membership, its own budget and its own program of work.[5]

It would, however, be a mistake to press the case for separatism far. If the United Nations is to be entrusted with greater responsibilities for international economic and technical assistance—as it must, for reasons previously considered—the members should see to it that the Organization is given power to assure effective coordination within the United Nations system of agencies.

There is much evidence of competing initiatives, overlapping activities, and proliferation of field offices and staff. For this situation member governments, including our own, are

[5] Statement by Dr. B. R. Sen to the U.N. Economic and Social Council, July 13, 1961, *Official Records* (32nd sess.), 1163rd mtng., July 13, 1961, para. 55.

to blame. Encouragement is often given to favored agencies to "go it alone," sometimes as a result of pressures by well-intentioned national groups. For example, the United States Department of Agriculture has exerted influence in support of the so-called "independence" of the Food and Agriculture Organization, with which it has close ties.

Thus, an earlier proposal to make use of U.S. food surpluses through the Food and Agriculture Organization would have assigned too much authority to that agency, without giving weight to the over-all responsibilities of the United Nations in the general field of economic development. The surplus food plan calls for the use of food, as well as finance, to assist in economic development; it would include such measures as allotting food as part of workers' pay, thus enlarging the capacity of the nation to give more employment, in addition to increasing the productivity of the workers themselves. Decisions involved in the administration of such a program, however, require coordination of its broad economic, social and industrial aspects. Accordingly, it was wise for the United States to join in sponsoring a resolution at the 1961 session of the General Assembly, providing for administration of the program by the United Nations, together with the Food and Agriculture Organization, under policy guidance of a Special Committee of twenty member nations.

Coordination of Operations

Much has been done through the machinery of the U.N. Administrative Committee on Coordination to deal with jurisdictional problems and to plan concerted action. The U.N. Technical Assistance Board, with its own Executive Chairman and secretariat, helps mount a combined attack on the problems of the less developed regions, and shows the advantage of strengthening a United Nations system as a whole. The Executive Chairman, a key official of the Central Secretariat, presides over a board on which Specialized Agencies are represented.

The United Nations Civilian Affairs Operation in the

Congo, about which books rather than headlines will one day be written, demonstrates how the agencies can work together, under the leadership of the United Nations, to provide essential services in a disordered society and check an impending slide into disaster. The Civilian Affairs Operation would not have been possible but for the participation of the Specialized Agencies. At the same time, the Secretary-General of the United Nations and the leadership which the United Nations Operation provided in the Congo enabled the Specialized Agencies to perform a maximum service.

As the Chief of Civilian Operation of the Congo, Dr. Sture Linner of Sweden, has reported, his mission's activities have touched "almost every aspect of the economic and social life of the Congo and . . . have played a substantial part in preventing vital public services from collapsing and putting some others on the road to recovery." The Civilian Operations staff, recruited within the space of a few months, has managed, among other things: to assure maintenance of the Congo's telephone and telegraph system; to establish channels of food supply and marketing within the interior areas of the country; and to maintain large refugee camps.

Assistance by the World Health Organization in the Congo has included rebuilding health services, restaffing hospitals, mobilizing emergency medical teams from twenty-four countries, controlling epidemics through water purification and immunization programs, recruiting 130 doctors to consult with and help develop indigenous medical services, and educating and training physicians. Although by mid-1961 there was still not a single Congolese medical graduate, it was the hope of the Director-General of W.H.O. that by the middle of 1963 about fifty qualified doctors of medicine would have returned to the Congo to play there a very important role, not only in the development of its medical services, but also in the socio-economic life of a country sadly short of university graduates.

Other United Nations services and agencies have likewise played an important role in the Congo. With respect to essential operations of government, the Specialized Agencies have provided economists and specialists in banking, taxation and other fields. Civil aviation and meteorological experts have been flown in to maintain commercial and military air operations. Agricultural, labor, judicial, educational, and social welfare specialists have been recruited to advise Congolese authorities in the development of these services. All these activities have been carried on in the midst of tumult and political conflict, at times threatening to engulf the very mechanism of stability itself.

The United Nations system of organizations and agencies has demonstrated capacity to carry out combined operations under difficult circumstances, provided that an adequate interagency institutional framework exists and leadership is forthcoming.

The U.N. Resident Representative

Experience in the Congo has, furthermore, demonstrated the value of the arrangement, now widely used in the United Nations Technical Assistance Program, of posting a United Nations Resident Representative in a nation where several U.N. agencies or services are working together.

The Executive Chairman of the Technical Assistance Board, David Owen, has steered the development of this institution from an experimental program in one country in 1950 to the present network circling the globe. The potential value of the system lies in coordinating the activities of the United Nations family of agencies at the country level and in aiding national governments to plan and administer their own economic and technical assistance programs.

In his last appearance before the Economic and Social Council, Secretary-General Hammarskjold admonished the heads of the Specialized Agencies, assembled in Geneva: "We should not be reluctant to entrust a single officer or a single unit with tasks on behalf of several agencies, or in the field of several agencies. Our resources are so meagre that we should neglect no opportunity to pool and stretch them." [6]

[6] Statement of July 13, 1961, Press Release ECOSOC/1387.

This wise advice suggests another useful role which Resident Representatives might fulfill in the interest of all members of the United Nations—that of cooperating with the local representatives of bilateral and regional programs, so as to assure the effectiveness of all undertakings within one country. In this connection, the Administrative Committee on Coordination has expressed the hope that ". . . the willingness of Governments to make increasing contributions to strengthen the impact of multilateral programmes will imply a readiness to conduct bilateral operations more and more within the multilateral framework of consultation and cooperation." [7]

Conclusion

The United States' national interest does not dictate any single approach to international economic cooperation. There are many things that can best be done through the United Nations system, and others that can be well done in close association with it. Certainly it is in our national interest to ensure that this international mechanism is strongly supported, and that it is fortified at the crucial points at which its healthy development is determined—particularly in its unique function of working closely with the governments of countries receiving aid from various outside sources.

Above all, we should not deprive the United Nations—under our leadership—of an opportunity to strengthen its influence over the newly developing nations, of promoting their sense of responsibility, and of fostering the elements of freedom and moderation present in all these nations, whose hands are held out for moral as well as material support.

[7] U.N. Economic and Social Council (32nd sess.), *Twenty-fifth Report of the Administrative Committee on Co-ordination,* E/3495 (1961), p. 17.

Chapter V

Financing the Structure for Peace

The difficulty of persuading nations to share in financing agencies essential to both keeping and building the peace, finds perennial confirmation in the struggle over the budget of the United Nations. The Organization will have begun to approach maturity when, as has been well said, members "give at least as much attention to the *policy* implications of *financial* decisions as they do to *financial* implications of *policy* decisions." [1]

One of the few binding decision-making powers conferred upon the General Assembly is approval of the budget and its apportionment among the members (Article 17). In 1946, the total expenditures of the United Nations, Specialized Agencies and special programs was less than $25 million, of which the United States contributed about $10 million. In 1961, the corresponding totals were $450 million and $194 million.[2]

Today, the Organization faces bankruptcy and there is no provision for a receivership. The Soviet government has extended the veto principle to all obligations which it finds uncongenial. In this, it is supported in important respects by France as, for example, by the latter's insistence that cost of

[1] J. David Singer, *Financing International Organizations* (The Hague: Nijhoff, 1961), pp. 176-177. And see the excellent study by John G. Stoessinger, *Financing the United Nations*, no. 535 of *International Conciliation*, November 1961.

[2] U.S. House, *United States Contributions to International Organizations*, Doc. No. 222, 87th Cong., 1st sess. (Washington: GPO, 1961), Table 23 and Appendix III.

military operations, such as those in the Congo, should be outside the regular budget and not subject to Assembly apportionment. So far as the Congo is concerned, French and Soviet recalcitrance is shared by Belgium, Portugal, the Union of South Africa and, needless to say, the Soviet echo-states in the United Nations. Most of the Arab states likewise participate in this exercise of selective security—largely to demonstrate consistency with their refusal to contribute to the upkeep of the U.N. Emergency Force in Gaza.

It is, of course, these very operations which create the threat of insolvency. By the end of 1961, a deficit of well over $100 million confronted the Organization. Acting Secretary-General U Thant warned the Fifth Committee of the General Assembly in December 1961 that within six months there would be a gap of $170 million between income and expenditures—a sum three times greater than the "regular budget" of the Organization.[3]

The regular budget, covering normal housekeeping, administrative and miscellaneous—though essential—institutions, such as the International Court of Justice, is usually covered with little difficulty, although some members have made an unenviable record of not meeting their obligations on time. In one particular field there has been a consistent effort on the part of some members to reduce an important function of the Organization. The Soviet bloc—with support from Britain, France, Belgium, and the Union of South Africa—has consistently desired to curb public information services. One sure evidence that the United Nations is neither "superstate" nor "world government" is its difficulty in securing funds for libraries and information centers—to say nothing of radio facilities —for the advancement of public knowledge concerning economic, political and social problems affecting the interests of the membership as a whole. The spirit of the iron curtain finds companionship with those who, for reasons of economy or disinterest, attach low priority to dissemination of information concerning the structure for peace.

[3] *The New York Times,* December 12, 1961.

Voluntary Programs and Emergency Operations

Many important programs of the Organization are covered by voluntary contributions on the part of member nations. Some of the most important of these—including the Special Fund, the High Commissioner for Refugees, the U.N. Relief and Works Agency for Palestine, UNICEF, and the Expanded Program for Technical Assistance—have been referred to above. Together, these accounted in 1961 for almost $150 million of the expenditures of the United Nations, that is to say, one-third of the total budget of all its agencies and programs.

There is an undeniable element of absurdity in approaching such programs as if they were charitable contributions to a community chest, rather than assessments for a community enterprise. Members of the United Nations, including those who demand special voting privilege as permanent members of the Security Council, declared in the Charter that "creation of conditions of stability and well-being" are "necessary for peaceful and friendly relations among nations" (Article 55). Furthermore, they pledged themselves to cooperate for the achievement of the purposes of that Article.

Hence, it is doubly disturbing to find both the Soviet Union and France demanding the installation of a separate "operational" budget, including economic and technical assistance programs, which would be subject to the will and whim of member states, rather than to apportionment by the General Assembly.

It must, nevertheless, be remembered that the United States was among those initially responsible for the distinction between the regular and "assessed" budget on the one hand, and the special or "voluntary" ones on the other. Some of the largest of these latter programs, such as the Children's Fund and the Refugee Programs, might not have come into existence at all had not the U.S. government been prepared to contribute on a scale far in excess of that which we felt appropriate for the regular budget of the Organization. Thus, in the early years of UNICEF the United States paid about 70 per

cent of its budget, though we were at the same time strenu-
ously urging the principle of a ceiling of $33\frac{1}{3}$ per cent upon
the contribution of any member to the United Nations
budget.[4] Although the United States was prepared to accept a
disproportionate financial burden for known emergencies, it
did not wish to make advance commitments for unpredictable
ones.

Major programs for economic assistance are now raised by
means of an annual rite called the "pledging conference." A
target is set at a General Assembly session and on a fixed day
thereafter delegations come forward to announce their pledges.
In December 1960, the Assembly set a goal of $150 million.
When the sun set on the pledging day of October 17, 1961,
something less than $98 million of pledges had been fired at
the target. The United States offered $60 million, subject to
the condition that its contribution would not exceed 40 per
cent of the total. Hence, unless belated pledges can be coaxed
out of reluctant members, the U.S. share will drop to approximately $40 million.

Attempts have been made to set up special budgets for
emergency peace-keeping purposes, apportioned among members according to the scale of the regular budget. Following a
bitter debate, the General Assembly in 1956 adopted this principle with respect to the U.N. Emergency Force.[5] Notwithstanding the decision, large-scale defaults have occurred so
that by the end of 1961 almost one-fourth of the amounts
appropriated since 1957 for the UNEF ($94 million) remained
unpaid. A similar process, though at a higher level—both of
obligation and default—has taken place with respect to the
Congo operation. Clearly, if the will is lacking to share in the
burdens of common defense, the form in which the obligation
is cast makes little difference in the outcome. A "pledging conference" could scarcely have produced less impressive results
than these.

[4] This principle was eloquently defended in successive sessions of the
General Assembly by Senator Vandenberg (1946) and by Ambassador Adlai
Stevenson (1947).
[5] G.A. Resolution 1089 (XI), December 21, 1956.

Legal Authority of the Assembly

Controversies concerning the legal obligation of members to defray their assessed share of the expenses incurred in using United Nations armed forces, as in the Congo, raise fundamental questions as to the nature of the Organization itself.

The General Assembly is vested with broadly stated authority to apportion "the expenses of the Organization" (Article 17). There is no explicit qualification of this power. Indeed, suggestions made at the San Francisco Conference to detail budgetary procedures and methods of apportioning expenses were rejected. The general grant of power was regarded as "an extension to the international field of the fundamental principle of democratic government that the purse strings should be held by the most widely representative organ." [6]

At the same time the Security Council is endowed by the Charter with "primary responsibility for the maintenance of peace and security" (Article 24). Moreover, the General Assembly is obliged by Article 11, paragraph 2, to refer to the Security Council any question relating to the maintenance of peace and security.

Consistently with its concept of "great-power unity," that is to say, of the right of a great power to veto substantive decisions of which it disapproves, the Soviet government contends that, by force of Articles 11 and 24, expenses directly connected with the maintenance of international peace and security are not subject to apportionment by the General Assembly.[7] Other members, including numerous American republics, likewise argue that assessment of such expenses does not fall within the scope of the Assembly's powers.

In order to dispel the legal fog which surrounds the vaguely formulated grant of the power of the purse, the Assembly has

[6] Secretary of State Edward R. Stettinius, Jr., "Report to the President on the Results of the San Francisco Conference" (June 26, 1945), in *The Charter of the United Nations,* Hearings before the Senate Committee on Foreign Relations, 79th Cong., 1st sess., July 9-13, 1945 (Washington: GPO, 1945; rev.), p. 65.

[7] G.A. (16th sess.), *Review of the Activities and Organization of the Secretariat,* A/4776 (June 14, 1961), para. 151.

wisely resolved to request the International Court of Justice for an Advisory Opinion which would interpret the Charter in this respect. If the Court were to accede to such a request, its Opinion might well entail a highly illuminating analysis of the basic nature and purposes of the Organization, as well as the constitutional relationship between the General Assembly and the Security Council in the crucial function of keeping the peace.

An Advisory Opinion given by the Court is, of course, entitled to the highest respect. Nevertheless, it does not have legally compulsive effect, as does a judgment in a contentious proceeding between states. The latter may, pursuant to Article 94 of the Charter, be given effect by whatever measures the Security Council deems necessary.

Accordingly, it is appropriate to consider what coercive devices would be available in the event the Court should sustain the broad assessment powers of the Assembly. The only provision in the Charter directly relevant is Article 19, which deprives a member of voting rights in the General Assembly in the event its arrears equal or exceed its assessments due for the preceding two years. The Assembly may, however, permit such a member to vote if satisfied that the default is due to conditions beyond the member's control. Assuming that the General Assembly were to find it expedient to invoke Article 19 to debar a defaulter from voting, the coercive effect of such a penalty would, of course, depend entirely upon the significance attached by the offender to sitting voteless, though not voiceless, in that body. Presumably the same restriction would apply to the right of the member to vote in commissions or councils elected by the Assembly, although this is not explicitly stated.

Moreover, the provision does not apply to voting in the Security Council. Hence the Soviet Union, a leading defaulter, could retain its veto power unimpaired.

Accordingly, it must be concluded regretfully that if the Organization is, in the end, to be preserved from insolvency, it will not be through the sheriff's writ, so much as by the slow-grinding court of public opinion.

Methods of Obtaining Revenue

As a means of creating or marshaling such public opinion, numerous devices have been suggested for raising the revenues of the United Nations. These include: allocation to the Organization of income derived from exploitation of Antarctic or submarine minerals; levying of various types of international taxation; appropriation by member states of a fixed percentage of gross national product or of funds now diverted to armaments, which would serve humanity better as a special International Fund for Peace and Security, or the like.

All such suggestions have a laudable objective. None would appear to be practicable in the absence of a will on the part of members to see the Organization work in accordance with its intended purposes. And, if such a will existed, it is difficult to see why the United Nations today should be threatened with insolvency.

One large-scale stopgap is the resolution adopted by the General Assembly in December 1961, authorizing a long-term, low-interest bond issue, to be subscribed by governments or approved lending institutions. Its purpose is, of course, to meet the deficits incurred in the UNEF and Congo military operations, by reason of the default of members in meeting these obligations. Such a device would be expected to prevent financial collapse before the General Assembly session in the fall of 1962, barring unforeseen additional crises which might well arise prior to that time.

The Soviet Union, as is to be expected, opposes the procedure in principle, professing to see in it dangers of placing a "mortgage" on the Organization. This ground of objection is patently fraudulent. No such contention was made by the Soviet Delegation, or any one else, in 1948 when the United Nations accepted a thirty-year loan of $65 million from the United States in order to finance construction of United Nations Headquarters in New York.

The actual motive underlying the Soviet objection to the loan doubtless is based upon its most promising aspect: the provision that it is to be repaid out of the regular assessed budget. It was for this reason that France joined the Soviet bloc in voting against the proposal. It is for this reason, also, that the loan may be called a healthy palliative, moving in the direction of giving life to the principle that "the purse strings should be held by the most widely representative organ."

Chapter VI

Human Rights, Self-Determination and the Domestic Jurisdiction

The "tumultuous and scandalous" aspects of General Assembly processes, in the phrase of President de Gaulle, are similar to those which have characterized the emergence of democratic societies, manifested notably in the French popular assemblies of the time of the Revolution and not entirely unknown since. Readjustment of social forces creates new leadership groups, which demand a share in decision-making, if not a monopoly of power. It is a process taking place within many of the new states themselves. The United Nations in this respect, as in others, reflects the ferment and dislocations of a changing world.

In order to help just demands find moderate channels, U.S. policy toward the United Nations should stress its primary function of assisting orderly *change* in the *status quo*, in contrast to the League of Nations' emphasis upon assuring orderly *maintenance* of the *status quo*. By making explicit the principles underlying U.S. use of the United Nations for the former purpose, we would thereby also expose the fraudulent character of Soviet pretensions of seeking just solutions though in fact exploiting unrest for its own sake.

Intelligible standards are needed for decisions concerning changes which justice and common sense demand. The essential commitment of the parties to the United Nations Charter, as of all international engagements, is to make honest judgments in specific situations. But a democratic society cannot measure its judgments against rubber yardsticks of policy.

This applies in particular to such problems high on the agenda of national concern of the new states as international protection of human rights and of self-determination.

Human Rights

In recent years, American attitudes toward the scope of United Nations action in the field of human rights have undergone barometric changes, reflecting heavy political weather at home, rather than "winds of change" abroad.

With regard to human rights treaties generally, some informed persons, although attributing value to pronouncements such as the Universal Declaration of Human Rights as standards for achievement, believe that enforceable codes or covenants would be illusory in view of the lawlessness of international society. Furthermore, there is reason to fear that support by the U.S. government of international protection of human rights might arouse hostility against the United Nations on the part of persons fearful lest domestic policies regarding civil rights might thus be exposed to international surveillance.[1]

Condemnation by the United States of genocide in Tibet or Hungary would have a more convincing ring if the United States were to ratify the Genocide Convention outlawing such practices. Although the U.S. government led efforts resulting

[1] Thus, John Foster Dulles, as Secretary of State, countered the Bricker Amendment to the Constitution of the United States—which would drastically curtail treaty-making power—by notifying the Senate in 1953 that the administration "would not at the moment press for ratification" of the Genocide Convention. At the same time, he felt constrained to voice a general doubt whether protection of human rights "is a proper area for treaty action." (*The Department of State Bulletin,* April 20, 1953, p. 580.) Mr. Dulles nevertheless had previously, while serving as a member of U.S. Delegations to the General Assembly, given vigorous leadership to efforts toward such treaties. For example, in 1948 he declared: "We must go on with the drafting of a Covenant which will seek to translate human rights into law." (*Three Years of the United Nations: Appraisals and Forecasts,* no. 445 of *International Conciliation,* November 1948, p. 585.)

in the conclusion of that treaty, which we signed in 1948, the Senate Foreign Relations Committee has never reported the treaty to the Senate.

The abandonment by the United States of support for enacting human rights into binding international legal obligations has arrested progress toward one important, though little noted, long-term objective: that of making individuals, as well as states, subjects of international law. The Genocide Convention moves toward this goal by embodying the concept of an international penal tribunal, even though the Convention does not of itself establish such a tribunal.[2] Mr. Dulles, testifying in 1948 before the House Foreign Affairs Committee on the relations of the United States to the United Nations, said: "I have believed for a long time that law only operates effectively if it relates to individuals rather than to states. . . . because it has been demonstrated time and time again that the corporate body, the state, is not a very reliable subject of law."[3]

The corollary principle, of equal importance, is to give individuals the right of recourse to international tribunals for remedies against prescribed international wrongs. Judge Philip C. Jessup has said: "No less wonderful than sputnik is the launching of the European Court of Human Rights under the Rome Convention."[4] Hyperbole aside, there is a basic truth in the parallel between man's pioneer reaches into space and his first efforts to chart a practical course in the elusive realms of human rights and freedoms.

[2] Genocide Convention, Article VI: "Persons charged with genocide . . . shall be tried by a competent tribunal of the State in the territory of which the act was committed, or by such international penal tribunal as may have jurisdiction with respect to those Contracting Parties which shall have accepted its jurisdiction." Controversy concerning the propriety—and even legality—of the trial of Eichmann by the Israeli government dramatically confirms the importance of having available a regularly constituted international penal tribunal, competent to try defined crimes.

[3] *Structure of the United Nations and the Relations of the United States to the United Nations,* Hearings before the House Committee on Foreign Affairs, 80th Cong., 2d sess., May 4-14, 1948 (Washington: GPO, 1948), pp. 288-289.

[4] "A Half-Century of Efforts to Substitute Law for War," Address before the Hague Academy of International Law, August 2, 1960, in *Report on the Fiftieth Anniversary of the Carnegie Endowment for International Peace* (New York: Author, 1961), p. 45.

On July 2, 1961, the European Court of Human Rights handed down the first judgment of an international court in a dispute concerning an issue between an individual and his own government.[5] In reporting the decision, a Dublin newspaper particularly noted that "the seven judges and the registrar wore the badge of Europe on their black robes—a circle of twelve golden stars on blue silk pinned to their shoulder." [6] It is not easy to imagine a symbol more pregnant with meaning for the struggle toward community and the rule of law than the badge of Europe affixed to the robe of a judge.

Self-Determination and Colonialism

Woodrow Wilson gave expression to the principle that "governments derive all their just powers from the consent of the governed," [7] at a time when one-third of the world's population was under some form of alien rule. Colonial enterprise often has transformed desert into farmland and mountain into mineral, but no colonial alchemy has ever yet been able to convert subjugated peoples into happy partners.

Two wars, radical social change, new technology and, above all, doctrines of individual rights and freedoms—often fostered by the governors themselves—have given the spirit of nationalism a volcanic force which can neither be resisted nor denied. Its explosive quality is generated not merely by a sense of political suppression or economic exploitation, which indeed in many cases does not exist. Domination of alien races has

---

[5] *Lawless v. Government of Ireland.* Mr. Lawless complained that he had been detained for five months without the opportunity to appear before a judge. The Court held this to be a violation of Article 5 of the Rome Convention, requiring that persons arrested or detained "shall be brought promptly before a judge . . . and shall be entitled a trial within a reasonable time." The Court nevertheless dismissed the complaint, on the ground that the action of the government was excused by Article 15, reserving to the parties the right to deal with "public emergency threatening the life of the nation."

[6] *The Irish Independent,* July 3, 1961.

[7] Address to the Senate of the United States, *Congressional Record,* v. 54, pt. 2, January 22, 1917, p. 1742.

inevitably been attended by racial or cultural discrimination, however covert.

This was the unspoken major premise upon which was grounded the indictment by twenty-nine Asian and African governments at the 1955 Bandung Conference: "Colonialism in all its manifestations is an evil which should speedily be brought to an end. The subjection of peoples to alien subjugation, domination and exploitation constitutes a denial of human rights. . . ."

It would be a mistake to dismiss this as demagogy or anti-Westernism. The roll call included allies of the United States —Japan, the Philippines, Thailand, Iran and Liberia, to say nothing of a member of the NATO alliance itself, Turkey. When Western statesmen complain against disparaging uses of the term "colonialism," they justly call attention to the accomplishments made and benefits conferred by many enlightened rulers, trustees and mandatories. The fact remains that European and Asian spokesmen conceive of the term differently, attaching to it meanings which are literally worlds apart.

Crosscurrents and conflicts attending the transition from one era to another involve threats to the peace as grave as those likely to arise from any other source of tension. Remaining hard-core colonial problems generate explosive force not merely because inexorable pressures for freedom meet resistance but—what is more dangerous—they often encounter a lack of capacity, rather than mere reluctance, on the part of the ruling power to find fair and practicable means of disengagement.

The liquidation of the British Empire, although accelerated by war and resistance, was successful essentially because of the character of British society itself. States inevitably project into their dealings with others the characteristics of their own domestic societies. It is an axiom particularly relevant to the relations between metropolitan powers and their dependencies. Authoritarian governments, such as those of Portugal and Spain, cannot find the capacity to grant to subject peoples freedom of the vote, or other basic civil liberties, when such rights are denied to citizens of the home countries.

Extreme examples of the working of this law of political behavior are, of course, the Soviet Union in Eastern Europe and Red China in Tibet. As former Secretary of State George C. Marshall once warned the General Assembly: "Governments which systematically disregard the rights of their own people are not likely to respect the rights of other nations and other people and are likely to seek their objectives by coercion and force in the international field."

This simple truth charges the future of Angola and Mozambique with potentialities of disaster. Similar dangers, and for like reasons, arise out of the conduct of the Union of South Africa in the mandated Territory of Southwest Africa. The International Court of Justice is now seized of a case testing whether the application of the policy of *apartheid* in the Territory is consistent with the mandate requirement to "promote to the utmost the material and moral well-being and the social progress of the inhabitants. . . ." It appears inevitable that, when the Union ceases this infamous policy in the Territory, irresistible demands will arise within the Union itself for the acceptance of elemental principles of human rights and freedoms.

With regard to a totally different type of colonial problem, that of Algeria, what is required of France is not so much relinquishment of control over a possession, as it is greater capacity of the French society to discipline domestic forces of extremism, which obstruct orderly solution to other problems as well.

The hard-core problems of colonialism are also rendered more complex by reason of the desire of some states to annex areas now under the government of others, the old question of irreconcilable territorial claims the world has had with it since organized political communities have existed.[8]

Perhaps the greatest obstacles of all to orderly transition to the new age are the often tragic gaps between political aspira-

---

[8] Examples are: Argentine claim to Falkland Islands; Indonesian claim to "West Irian"; Guatemalan and Mexican claims regarding British Honduras; Yemen's claim to Aden. The Indian claim to Goa was, of course, one of the most vigorously pressed, ending in its forcible seizure in December 1961.

tion on the one hand, and economic weakness and social instability on the other. When, as in the case of the Congo, seventy-five years of colonial rule abruptly end, with only seventeen university graduates produced in the entire country, a legacy of chaos is inevitable. The burdens thrust upon the international community, including the United States, make it a matter of mere common sense to keep a watchful eye on areas of incipient disaster such as Angola, Ruanda-Urundi, or other places which are winding their tragic way into the headlines.

The dilemmas faced by the United States in deciding upon a course in disputes concerning self-determination, such as the foregoing, are often described as that of having to choose between "loyalty to our tradition," and "loyalty to our friends," particularly our NATO allies. That is too simple and clearcut a way to describe the situation, though the dilemma may nonetheless be a real one. In controversies between dependent peoples and democratic ruling societies, there will inevitably be forces of moderation active on both sides of the table.[9]

It should be an object of U.S. policy to identify such forces of moderation and to sustain them in efforts to find constructive solutions. Such a course on our part would no doubt provoke anguished cries of "intervention" or "meddling," particularly from extreme or ultranationalist elements on each side of the dispute. Yet, the traditional "hands-off" policy is illusory. When we deny aid and comfort to moderates, we stem the tide of history and strengthen extremism, whatever our intention may be.

Obviously, there will always be differences of opinion within our own country concerning the elements properly to be regarded as "moderate" or "extreme." Application of a policy of intervention for constructive ends calls for exercise of that rare quality of "impartiality of spirit and of judgment," which was Woodrow Wilson's conception of true neutrality. Never-

[9] This fact distinguishes such situations from those in which the ruling state has a totalitarian character, where "forces of moderation" find little place. Although Communist hegemony over captive nations may fairly be called "neocolonialism," it is, more accurately, a retrograde and despotic imperialism.

theless, there is no safe detour around the necessity for exercising such spirit and judgment, whether the dispute concerns Algeria, Angola, Southwest Africa or any other bitterly contested colonial struggle.

If the doctrine of self-determination is to be more than an abstraction, it must be given dimensions in time and in space. There must be some standard, however flexible, as to the group or the unit which is appropriate for the exercise of the right of self-determination in a particular case. Fragmentation and secession can be deadly enemies of order, without which "self-determination" becomes a mockery. Our own history proves this point. So does the evolution of the Congo since its independence.

Policies followed in the Congo by the majority of members of the United Nations, including the United States, have been based upon the Security Council resolution of February 21, 1961, which has been discussed in an earlier chapter. Application of these policies has included the positive aspects of shoring up a stricken economy, introducing the rudiments of governmental and social services, and making a start toward education of the Congolese people. These efforts, likewise, have been described above.

However, the application of U.N. Congo policy has also necessarily involved what might be called the "negative" function of averting evils even greater than those which already existed. It is, of course, never possible to prove a negative, to persuade the fearful or the skeptical of the disaster which merely "might have been." At least a minimal degree of confidence must be reposed in the judgment and probity of those responsible for policy-making, always assuming complete candor on their part concerning the facts and the dilemmas which confront them.

There can be no reasonable doubt that Balkanization of the Congo, particularly through secession of its principal source of revenue, would create a disaster. The fragments would require vast subsidies from abroad and would even then be exposed to subversion and conflict. Such a conflict could scarcely be contained, either as to place or as to parties.

In the face of such risks, and of the current and contingent burdens borne by others, notably the United States, it cannot fairly be contended that the course of events in the Congo may not legitimately be subjected to international processes. Argument that the "people of Katanga" have been deprived of their right of self-determination begs the very question at issue: is Katanga, or is the Congo as a whole, the appropriate unit for the exercise of the right? The overwhelming weight of opinion in the United Nations, including that of the United States, is that this question was settled when the constitution for the Congo was adopted, and a parliamentary regime installed, including representatives of the leading Katanga parties themselves. The *form* of unification is for decision by the Congolese people as a whole; the *principle* of unification must be protected from those who would destroy it by force, whether or not externally subsidized.

Whether the United Nations has the capacity to create standards and apply processes for dealing with such highly charged issues as these depends largely upon the loyalty with which members honor the Charter principles and the consistency with which they use the forum.

Fears that the United Nations is "finished," or that this many-footed organism is "on its last legs," have been voiced at numerous critical stages in the life of the Organization. The United Nations will survive not because its membership has the self-discipline needed to meet each crisis with an appropriate judgment or reaction—which it may or may not do—but because there is no practicable alternative to the United Nations, and nothing but chaos without it.

The Indian invasion of the Portuguese enclave of Goa in December 1961 provided a striking example of the latter fact, as well as of the inconsistency of a member state both with respect to the principles of the Charter and the uses of the Organization. In that case, as in that of Kashmir, India has accorded a higher priority to a unilaterally professed "right of self-determination" than to the Charter principles enjoining the use or threat of force. The fallacy lies in its insistence upon applying both principles upon its own terms, thus presuming to act as judge in its own cause.

In the case of Kashmir, which India itself had initially brought before the United Nations, it has ignored repeated urging by United Nations bodies and representatives to comply with internationally determined standards and procedures, designed to accord genuine self-determination to the people of Kashmir.

The government of Portugal sought instant and urgent redress from the Security Council for the wrong done in Goa. This was a wholly appropriate action for Portugal to take, and a striking example of the fact that there is no practical alternative to the Organization, which Portugal has, indeed, done so little to strengthen. Portugal has long been among the members refusing to help finance United Nations operations in the Congo. It has espoused the most rigid application of the principle of "domestic jurisdiction" in all issues of self-determination arising in the United Nations. It has supported the contention of the Union of South Africa that the Organization should not exercise a supervisory function over the Mandated Territory of Southwest Africa. It has refused to transmit information to the United Nations relative to its dependent territories, thus violating its commitment under Article 73(e) of the Charter.

Portugal's course in these matters does not vindicate the Indian government's aggression against Goa nor give it a defense against Portugal's just complaint. The Indian action in Goa and the general policy of Portugal in the United Nations do, however, exemplify an all-too-common inconsistency on the part of member states regarding the nature and uses of the Organization.

Members of the United Nations are often—and with reason —criticized for applying a double standard of morality as, for example, in withholding condemnation of Soviet imperialism while clamoring for freedom of areas governed under ancient colonial charters, even where civil liberties and economic reforms have been genuine concerns of the governors. Nevertheless, there is an element of unreality in expecting this voluntary assemblage of sovereign states to respond with a "collective morality" only at such times or on such occasions as it may suit the wishes or interests of particular members. The

United Nations battery can generate no greater moral power than that with which it is charged by the membership. The Organization cannot be expected to cope with crisis, if the Charter is deformed into an instrument for selective—rather than collective—security.

Domestic Jurisdiction

Expansion of international protection of human rights and self-determination, as called for by the Charter, poses constitutional dilemmas for members, including the United States, which are traditionally jealous to protect their sovereignty from foreign encroachment. The dilemma is focused by the "domestic jurisdiction" clause of the Charter.[10]

In opposing the Bricker Amendment, the late Secretary of State Dulles remarked that "the test of any Constitution is not the way it reads but the way it works." [11] In fact, Article 2(7) reads one way, Article 10 another. The latter Article empowers the Assembly to discuss and recommend with respect to "any questions or any matters within the scope of the present Charter." The "scope" of the Charter is necessarily broad. Moreover, what constitutes "intervention" within the meaning of Article 2(7) has been the basis of frequent dialectical exercises in the forum.[12]

At the San Francisco Conference, the four sponsoring governments (United States, United Kingdom, U.S.S.R. and China) authorized a Joint Statement [13] rejecting proposals to

[10] Article 2(7): "Nothing contained in the present Charter shall authorize the United Nations to intervene in matters which are essentially within the domestic jurisdiction of any state. . . ."

[11] Statement before the Senate Judiciary Committee (April 6, 1953), *The Department of State Bulletin*, April 20, 1953, p. 595.

[12] Questions have arisen whether the following actions constitute "intervention": (1) Inclusion of an item on an agenda; (2) recommendations, either in general or addressed to a particular state; (3) establishment of study commissions, such as one to report upon the racial situation in South Africa. In virtually every case, the Assembly, despite objection, has taken the action proposed or a reasonable approximation thereof. (See *Repertory of United Nations Practice* [New York: United Nations, 1955], v. 1, pp. 130-135, and v. 2, pp. 56-59.)

[13] *Documents of the United Nations Conference on International Or-*

give an explicit definition to "domestic jurisdiction." The statement pointed out that "international law is subject to constant change and therefore escapes definition. It would, in any case, be difficult to define whether or not a given situation comes within the domestic jurisdiction of a State. In this era the whole internal life of a country is affected by foreign conditions. . . ." The corollary of the last-quoted sentence is that "foreign conditions" likewise must be affected by the "whole internal life" of a state. The traditional analysis of "domestic jurisdiction" is less willing to concede that anything which happens at home could be of legitimate concern to others. A state could hardly hoard its own sovereignty as a national treasure, yet claim the right to dip into its neighbor's stockpile.

A concept of sovereignty which recognizes that its essence is not diminished by reason of being shared for a common purpose does not underestimate the importance of "sovereignty." It merely assigns it a different function: that of serving as a *means,* rather than as an *end,* of national interest.

The difference in approach is not mere verbalism. It leads to clashes, within and between nations, concerning the policies to be pursued on many crucial issues. These include treatment by states of their own nationals—one of the perennials of the United Nations landscape,[14] violations of human rights by the Communist governments in Eastern Europe, colonial issues, treatment by states of foreign property, and—of particular significance in the case of the United States—attitudes toward use of the International Court of Justice and the development of the "rule of law."

ganization, San Francisco, 1945, v. 6: *Commission I: General Provisions* (London and New York: U.N. Information Organizations, 1945), p. 507.

14 The question of race conflict in the Union of South Africa has been before the United Nations since 1952 and appears to be generating continually more explosive international tensions. Thus, the Assembly has, by overwhelming majorities, registered its conviction that the policy of *apartheid* "constitutes a grave threat to the peaceful relations between ethnic groups in the world" (G.A. Resolution 820 [IX]). The Security Council on April 1, 1960, requested the Secretary-General to visit the Union, to seek ways to moderate international tensions inflamed by the Sharpeville killings.

Chapter VII

The Rule of Law

The people of the United States are often favored with flights of oratory extolling the "rule of law" among the nations, but practical action to achieve it has largely remained grounded. One reason is a lack of agreement as to the meaning of the phrase. Is it an objective, a program of action, or merely a slogan?

Facile and sometimes misleading analogies are drawn to highly developed legal systems, with resulting confusion between cause and effect. It is erroneously assumed that the disordered condition of the world results from the absence of codes, courts and constabulary. A clearer perspective might be gained by approaching the matter just the other way round.

The lack of rules and the inadequacy of machinery for cooperation are surely symptoms, rather than causes. They reflect almost total absence of prime prerequisites of any legal system: an organized will and a moral purpose. Except upon such foundations, a legal order cannot be created without recourse to unacceptable devices of coercion.

In an age balanced on the edge of terror and the rim of space, oversimplified solutions are hard to resist. World government proposals are alluring, though they focus too much upon mechanisms of order, without giving heed to the political and moral fuel needed for motive power. Likewise, some are drawn to ethical abstractions, such as "moral rearmament," which stress good intentions but ignore the mechanisms needed in order to bring moral forces to bear in specific cases.

The function of the lawyer is to help identify the circles of common interest which exist in a close-knit world of sovereign states. His task is to define the principles and institutions by which those common interests may be furthered. It is in these practical and specific ways that he can help forge a sense of "community," which remains a mere literary expression unless it reflects a sense of common interest and a capacity for self-discipline.

There are many, and often unsuspected, areas of common interest, even between East and West. Some "law" already exists; more can be developed. Examples include rules of the road for sea and airways; the agreement, to which both the United States and Soviet Union are parties, prohibiting militarization of Antarctica; and the agreement, reached during the 1961 session of the General Assembly, to continue the United Nations Committee of the Peaceful Uses of Outer Space, upon which both governments sit. The United States and the Soviet Union have concurrently condemned stationing, orbiting or testing weapons in outer space.

The emergence of new states likewise offers wide opportunities for American cooperation in helping develop concepts and scope of international law, and in training indigenous lawyers and administrators. The United Nations is an excellent vehicle for this purpose, enriched and supplemented by the work of private institutions, such as American law schools and bar associations, which have already begun programs to provide consultants, teachers, libraries and educational materials.

The United States should, above all, take a lead in extending the rule of law among like-minded nations. One practical way in which to give greater dimension to the Atlantic community would be to move forward to a well-developed rule of law among its members, including increased resort to the International Court of Justice. The Western European nations, with their growing common institutions and their Court of Human Rights, are already on that road.

Indeed, it is difficult to envisage a "concert of free nations" without the sinews of common legal principles and a common will to further legal processes in their mutual dealings. By becoming a "rule-of-law bloc," the free nations could lead the way toward a just order by practice as well as expound it by precept.

The responsible role for lawyers toward the same end involves application of their skills and experience in development of new standards and procedures for keeping peace. They can help find more effective ways to use existing institutions, such as the United Nations and the International Court of Justice, and expose demagogic or illusory formulas. As community leaders, and in their associations, lawyers can further public understanding that national self-interest is rooted in the common interest of all nations in a just peace.[1]

The American Bar Association, so long governed by obsolescent attitudes toward the working requirements of a rule of law, has at last begun to emerge into the twentieth century. The membership no longer responds with acclaim to laments such as that voiced by a past president of the Association, that "the Socialists and Communists and the International planners and do-gooders"—working through the United Nations— were intent upon creating a "world law which would be superior to and override the domestic laws of the member states, including the United States." [2]

More recently, another past president of the Association, Charles S. Rhyne, has been chairing a "Special Committee on World Peace Through Law," which has sponsored meetings of leading lawyers, at home and abroad, seeking ways to make more effective use of international processes and to develop principles and working legal rules to govern the increasingly complex political, economic and cultural relations among nations.

It is an effort which recognizes the need for progress by means of education rather than incantation. The latter too often characterized attitudes of the American legal community during the interwar years. On the one side were the isolation-

---

[1] For an excellent discussion, see the essay by Louis Henkin, "Toward a 'Rule of Law' Community," in *The Promise of World Tensions,* edited by Harlan Cleveland (New York: Macmillan, 1961).

[2] Frank E. Holman, "To Save the Constitution," *The Freeman* (March 1955), pp. 360-361.

ists, voicing primordial fears of "planners and do-gooders." On the other side were those who, in the succinct expression of Judge Jessup, "sought to strengthen the conventional outlawry of war by fervent assertion of its effectiveness."[3] The world now stands one generation and a devastating world war beyond the Kellogg-Briand Treaty of 1928 and other unstructured efforts of that period to "outlaw" war by mere convention and exhortation.

Few informed persons today would confuse bare legalism with the rule of law. Nonetheless, the U.S. government and people continue to indulge the hope that if we loudly hail the United Nations as the "cornerstone" of our foreign policy, that suffices to make it a keystone of the structure for peace. A prime example of lag between precept and practice may be found in American attitudes toward the use of the International Court of Justice.

The International Court of Justice

The history of the Resolution [4] by which the Senate consented to the U.S. Declaration accepting the compulsory jurisdiction of the International Court of Justice involved the application, in rapid succession, of two mutually contradictory approaches toward the use of the Court.

The Senate Foreign Relations Committee had given careful consideration to the question whether it should be for the Court, or for parties to a dispute, to decide whether a particular case is within the jurisdiction of the Court. On July 25, 1946, under Senator Connally's chairmanship, the Committee unanimously recommended favorable action upon a resolution reflecting the principle that such a decision should be left to the Court, rather than to a party.[5] The report of the

[3] "A Half-Century of Efforts to Substitute Law for War," Address before the Hague Academy of International Law, August 2, 1960, in *Report on the Fiftieth Anniversary of the Carnegie Endowment for International Peace* (New York: Author, 1961), p. 42.

[4] S. Resolution 196, 79th Cong., 2d sess., August 2, 1946.

[5] *International Court of Justice,* Report no. 1835 of the Senate Committee on Foreign Relations, 79th Cong., 2d sess. (Washington: GPO, 1946).

Committee dealt with the matter in detail, and explained its reasoning as follows:

> The question of what is properly a matter of international law is, in case of a dispute, appropriate for decision by the Court itself, since if it were left to the decision of each individual state, it would be possible to withhold any case from adjudication on the plea that it is a matter of domestic jurisdiction. It is plainly the intention of the statute that such questions should be decided by the Court. . . . The Committee therefore decided that a reservation of the right of decision as to what are matters essentially within domestic jurisdiction *would tend to defeat the purposes which it is hoped to achieve by means of the proposed declaration.* . . . [Italics added.]

Nevertheless, when the resolution reached the Senate floor, that body, still responding to Senator Connally's leadership, accepted his suddenly introduced Amendment,[6] which did precisely what his Committee had warned against doing just one week before; that is, it reserved to the United States the very right which tended "to defeat the purposes" of the Declaration.

Much has been written for and against repeal of the Connally Amendment, but it is difficult to improve upon the cogent brevity of the reasons set forth in the above-quoted report of Senator Connally and his colleagues.

With regard to procedures which might be adopted in future by the United States on this matter—assuming the Connally Amendment is not repealed—it is important to remember that, under our Constitution, the President is charged with the conduct of foreign relations. Accordingly, the executive, not the legislative branch, has the constitutional authority to make the determination envisaged in the Connally Amendment. Rather than following the dubious precedent of the Interhandel case,[7] the Department of State should act on the

---

[6] ". . . Provided, that such declaration shall not apply to— . . . b. disputes with regard to matters which are essentially within the domestic jurisdiction of the United States *as determined by the United States.*" (Italics added.) The underlined words constitute the "Connally Amendment." The debate in the Senate is reported in the *Congressional Record*, v. 92, pt. 8, August 1-2, 1946; see particularly p. 10695.

[7] Switzerland v. United States [1959] I.C.J. Rep. 6. The United States

basis that the Amendment in no sense *requires* the executive to exercise the right reserved by the Amendment.

If a legitimate doubt as to jurisdiction does arise, the executive should follow the practice, recommended by the Foreign Relations Committee itself, of remitting the question to the Court for decision. There is no reason why the executive should insist upon exercising a discretion which the Senate Foreign Relations Committee itself unanimously thought should be left to the Court.

Insistence upon keeping the key to the courthouse in our pocket is strangely out of keeping with the traditional American respect for the judicial process as the prime guarantor of the rule of law. The inconsistency, shared by most other states as well, is due in large part to the fact that the major sources of international tension involve political, economic and other "nonjusticiable" elements. Even where interrelated legal questions could be cleared away by submission to the Court, states are reluctant to risk adverse decision by a tribunal.[8]

Resort to the Court and confidence in the Court are mutually reinforcing. If importance is attached to judicial settlement—as it should be—the Court will be found to merit respect. Experience has shown that use of the Court can be facilitated by treaty provisions whereby parties agree to submit to the Court any dispute concerning application or interpretation of the treaty which has not been settled by negotiation. Such a "compromissory" clause was included in the mandate agreements after World War I, and is the basis for jurisdiction in a pending case involving the administration by the Union of South Africa of the Territory of Southwest Africa.

The United States has not only been apathetic toward use

determined that the disposition by this government of assets vested by the Alien Property Custodian was essentially within our domestic jurisdiction, hence beyond the Court's powers.

[8] Obvious examples are: failure of Israel and Egypt to submit to the Court basic legal issues involved in the Suez dispute; refusal of the Soviet Union to submit *any* question to the Court, even one such as Berlin, where it contends a major legal shift has occurred in the basis of the occupation; and Red China's dispute with India concerning sovereignty over border areas.

of the International Court of Justice. It has likewise failed to exert leadership in the twenty-one-member International Law Commission, the function of which is to promote "the progressive development of international law and its codification." [9]

The representation of the United States on the Commission in recent years, has been inexpert. Yet, among the topics selected by the Commission for codification are, for example, the law of treaties, arbitral procedure, regime of the high seas and territorial waters, treatment of aliens, rights of asylum, and many other problems of consequence to the national interest. It has been suggested that the Commission be so organized as to sit continuously, instead of in short sessions as at present.

The Legal Committee of the General Assembly is normally assigned items of minor consequence, and only a few of these. There is little thought given to the formulation of new principles of law, despite the growing interdependence of nations, the spread of trade and investment, and the increased importance attached to the protection of human rights and freedoms.

The U.S. government's relative lack of interest in these matters perhaps reflects reluctance on the part of the executive branch to arouse the latent hostility of segments of Congress—particularly those from southern states—to international action in fields which traditionally have been regarded as "domestic." Such hostility is no doubt a political fact of life to be reckoned with, but, unless it is faced candidly by those who espouse the "rule of law," their eloquence will inevitably be subject to discount.

[9] G.A. Resolution 174 (II), November 21, 1947; G.A.O.R. (2d sess.), *Resolutions, 16 September–29 November 1947*, A/519 (1948), p. 105.

Chapter VIII

Conclusion

The functioning of the United Nations, like that of any instrument of cooperation, reflects widely divergent attitudes on the part of members concerning the relationship between national self-interest and the common interests of nations. On one extreme stand those who seek national security through traditional power politics and tend to regard common interest and self-interest as mutually exclusive. On the other extreme are those few who would subordinate national interest to an amorphous "general interest," often papered over with abstractions, such as "world conscience" or "world opinion."

Neither extreme viewpoint gives due weight to the implicit connection between self-*interest* and self-*discipline*. It was this practical relationship to which De Tocqueville referred when he described "self-interest rightly understood" as men's "chief remaining *security against themselves*." [1] Too narrow a conception of self-interest undermines the capacity for self-discipline, which is needed for cohesion in even the most rudimentary "community." Self-discipline generates moral forces enabling societies to define their responsibilities courageously and to pursue their interests wisely.

In a climate of frustration it is forgotten that the responsibilities of the United States were not born in San Francisco or dreamed up in Washington. The circles of our common interests with other nations are concentric, overlapping—and constantly shifting. These interests can best be advanced through

---

[1] Alexis de Tocqueville, *Democracy in America* (1835), Second Book, Chapter VIII.

participation in organizations both universal and regional in scope, never forgetting that the backbone of foreign policy must always remain the wise use of "good old-fashioned diplomacy."

Accordingly, it is important carefully to appraise suggested "alternatives" to the United Nations which may, in effect, be little more than exercises in wish fulfillment. Although world government offers "challenging theories and ideas," as Dag Hammarskjold once remarked, "the political realities with which we live, rooted as they are deep in the disparate histories and cultures of many peoples, make this course impracticable in the foreseeable future." [2]

On the other hand, some who feel that the United Nations has proved too weak a reed, urge "reliance" upon a strengthened Atlantic community. This estimate is true, at least for the short range, in such vital matters as organizing for defense. However, it would be a mistake to assume that no scope remains for universal as well as regional agencies in the endless struggle toward a just order. There is nothing incompatible between forging closer bonds among Atlantic nations, linked to each other in spirit and in interest, while at the same time seeking to strengthen more general processes for dealing with problems—political, social, and economic—in which common interests of the Atlantic community merge with the interests of other nations and societies. The weaknesses of the United Nations spring from many of the same difficulties which beset the members of the Atlantic community, and smaller nations in all parts of the world share in many of their dilemmas. Moreover, problems arise involving divergent interests among members of the community, and these can often be dealt with best in a wider forum. Examples are, of course, Suez, Cyprus and the Congo.

When the Soviet government, in the fall of 1960, invited the late Secretary-General to resign "in a chivalrous manner," Mr. Hammarskjold at once turned to the small nations. "The Organization is first of all *their* Organization," he said. "I

2 "The Vital Role of the United Nations in a Diplomacy of Reconciliation," *United Nations Review*, May 1958, p. 6.

shall remain in my post . . . as long as *they* wish me to do so." [3] The Secretary-General did not, of course, mean that the big powers should abdicate their responsibilities or interests, or that the Organization should, so to speak, be "turned over" to the small states. He was reminding the entire membership that no power, however great, may deprive the weaker of the shelter of the Charter or a voice in matters of general concern.

The United States runs the risk of nourishing bystander attitudes on the part of the smaller nations when we ourselves characterize major world problems as "cold war issues." [4] Such an approach rests upon a dual fallacy: that issues of vast import, such as disarmament, ever truly have an "outcome"; and that the shifting impact of such problems is unconnected with the "opinion" of others as well as with the opinion of the great powers themselves.

The possibility that there may be an opportunity for fruitful negotiations should always be probed, and there is always hope that specific crises can be resolved. But the American people must be prepared to believe, and live with the belief, that major controversies will continually arise in varied and unpredictable forms.

Crises may end; problems merely change shape. And the shape they take will be affected by the opinions which the people of the United States are able to bring to bear upon world events. "Opinion is power," said Jefferson. Moral force does not move mountains, but it moves men to action, and by their action mountains can be moved—and civilizations built or destroyed. That is the danger, and promise, of the New Age of the Atom and the Individual.

[3] Statement to the General Assembly, October 3, 1960, Press Release SG/966. (The italics are Mr. Hammarskjold's.)

[4] Thus, for example, Assistant Secretary of State Harlan Cleveland, "The Road Around Stalemate," *Foreign Affairs*, October 1961, p. 29: "The great cold war issues . . . are questions whose outcome may be more important to the great powers than considerations of world opinion. Berlin is certainly in this class. So is nuclear disarmament. So, too, is the continuing problem of Communist China and its relationship to the world community."

"*Pioneer for a New Age*"

Shortly after assuming the Office of Secretary-General in 1953, Dag Hammarskjold concluded an address with a credo and a prophecy:

No one can foresee with certainty what will emerge from the give and take of the forces at work in any age. For that reason history often seems to run its course beyond the reach of any man or nation. We cannot mold the world as masters of a material thing. Columbus did not reach the East Indies. But we can influence the development of the world from within, as a spiritual thing. In this sense, Columbus would have been a pioneer for a new age even if he himself had never reached America.

. . . And Dag Hammarskjold never reached Ndola . . .

Index

Acting Secretary-General, *see* Thant, U
Aden, 109 *n.*
African states, 9, 52, 64, 108
Albania, 63
Algeria, 50, 109
Alliance for Progress, 85
American Bar Asso., 118
Angola, 109, 110
Antarctica, 117
Argentina, 109 *n.*
Armstrong, Hamilton Fish, 9, 47 *n.*
Asian states, 9, 52, 64, 108
Atomic Energy Comm., 61
atomic radiation studies, 27
Austin, Warren R., 77

Bandung Conference, 108
Belgium, 97
Belgrade Conference, 9, 67
Bricker Amendment, 105
British Honduras, 109 *n.*
Bulgaria, 63, 64 *n.*
Byrnes, James F., 63 *n.*

Cambodia, 27
Central Treaty Organization (CENTO), 50
China, People's Republic of, 45, 52, 58, 61-2, 64, 65, 88, 109
Churchill, Winston S., 3, 41
coexistence, 4
Cole, Sterling, 91
collective security, 6, 7, 42-3, 46-51, 59-61
Colombo Plan, 85
colonialism, 107-15
Comm. for Conventional Armaments, 61
Congo (Léopoldville), 15, 19, 28, 34-7, 51 *n.*, 52, 76, 78, 92-4, 97, 102, 110, 111
Advisory Committee on, 29, 35-6
Connally Amendment, 119-20
Connally, Tom, 42, 119-20
Crimea Conference, 41
Cuba, 9
Cyprus, 50